IN SEARCH OF

Essays from a new Scottish Open-plan Primary School

DAVID HAMILTON

The Scottish Council for Research in Education

SCRE Publication 68

Now published by the Scottish
Council for Research in
Education, 15 St. John Street,
Edinburgh, EH8 8JR.

ISBN 0 901116   (boards)
ISBN 0 901116 65 3 (limp)

Copyright © 1977 The Scottish Council for Research in Education. All rights reserved. No part of this publication may be reproduced or transmitted in any form or by any means, electronic or mechanical, including photocopy, recording, or any information storage and retrieval system, without permission in writing from the publisher.

Printed and bound in Great Britain for Hodder and Stoughton Educational, a division of Hodder and Stoughton Ltd, Mill Road, Dunton Green, Sevenoaks, Kent, by Lindsay & Co Ltd, 17 Blackfriars Street, Edinburgh, EH1 1ND.

CONTENTS

		Page
Preface		v
1.	Early One Morning (an Introduction)	1
2.	Becoming an Open-Plan School	8
3.	Open-Plan Schools Past and Present	23
4.	First Days at School	38
5.	The Case of the Missing Chairs	66
6.	All Work and No Play?	75
7.	Episodes of School Life.	82
8.	The Logic of the Open-Plan School	98
Bibliographic Note		108

FIGURES

1.	The Case-study Building (showing class bases for 1974-75)	5
2.	The Case-study Building (earliest published plans, 1972)	13

PREFACE

"Space is not merely a background for events but possesses an autonomous structure."

(Albert Einstein, *Physicist.*)[1]

In 1974 the Scottish Council for Research in Education published *Space for Learning*[2], a thirty-page account of recent developments in open-plan schooling in Scotland. As a piece of research, *Space for Learning* was committed to servicing a debate, not resolving it. It did not set out to test a range of pre-specified hypotheses or even to survey every aspect of open-plan schooling. Instead, it tried to respond in an accessible manner to some of the questions posed at that time by teachers and administrators.

In Search of Structure utilises a similar research perspective. It identifies the general phenomena of open-plan schooling and locates them in the day to day work of one school. As with *Space for Learning* its principal concern is to contribute—in a concise but sensitising manner—to wider discussions about the problems and possibilities of open-plan schooling.

Although the overall responsibility for this report necessarily rests with the author, its preparation would have been impossible without the cooperation and assistance of the following teachers, research colleagues and others:

C Adelman, A Ball, N Bennett, C Boag, D Boydell, R Boyes, J Brunton, C Clarke, P Clift, E Coghill, M Cookson, M Corrie, B Cuthbertson, C Darroch, J Dickie, M Dilbey, W B Dockrell, D Elliot, J Elliot, R Graham, H Forrester, I Fraser, M Fraser, A Hamilton, M Hamilton, J Henderson, G Hudson, M Jamieson, S Kemmis, P Kenley, S Kleinberg, G Lawrence, K MacIver, I McRiner, D Medd, J Moore, D Morrow, K Napier, M Reid, K Richmond, W Robertson, B Sanders, M Scrimgeour, E Smail, D Smith, J Smith, L Smith, M Stewart, G Thorpe, E Welsh, B Wise, R Young.

---

[1] R W Clark, *Einstein: The Life and Times* (London: Hodder & Stoughton, 1973), p 198.
[2] Malcolm Corrie, *Space for Learning* (Edinburgh: SCRE, 1976). See also M Corrie, "Open Plan Schools: Some Research Evidence", *Education in the North*, Vol. 13 (1976).

The author would also like to thank the Scottish Council for Research in Education for their sponsorship of this research; the Social Science Research Council for its financial assistance (Grant No HR 3455); and Reiach Hall & Lawrence for permission to reproduce architectural drawings.

Finally, this report is dedicated to the many pupils and parents who, often anonymously, contributed their experiences and insights.

1

EARLY ONE MORNING
(an Introduction)

"If structures exist it is up to the observer to elicit and analyse them."
(Jean Piaget, *Psychologist.*)[1]

Like many of her profession Mrs Barber teaches in a storeroom, a cloakroom and a corridor. Fortunately, her classroom incorporates all these features; it was deliberately planned that way as part of an open-plan primary school.

Mrs Barber's teaching space defies conventional description. It lacks the usual symmetry of doors and walls, front and back. When unoccupied—as in the school holidays—it comprises three distinct units: a *home base* rather like a large enclosed alcove; a *wet zone* shared with two other classes; and an intervening *class area* marked out by an irregular combination of external and internal walls. Small bay windows, stretches of cotton print curtains and lengths of built-in shelving help to add further visual interest to the design.

The walls, doors and ceilings also exhibit a variety of textures. The base and class areas are covered by a close-cropped nylon 'turf'; the wet zone is protected by plastic tiles; and overhead, almost within reach, are fluorescent lights and mottled accoustic ceiling tiles.

Mrs Barber's classroom furniture is varied in form but specialised in function. In the class area there are four mobile storage units, three moveable trestle tables, ten small tables, twenty-five chairs and three display screens. The wet zone contains two sinks, a fixed work-surface, a

---

[1] *Epistomologie des Science de l'Homme* (Paris: Gallimard, 1961), p 210.

work-bench with a vice, three double-sided easels, and two deep troughs for water or sand. The standard fixtures and fittings are completed by a brown chalk board, an upholstered arm chair and a variety of low soft seats.

During term time these furnishings are rendered more distinctive. Charts, painting and craft work break up the uniformity of the off-white walls, flowers and potted plants crowd out the window-sills, and screens and portable frames create special areas for display or project work.

Before the children arrive each day the teaching area begins to come to life. The chalkboard marks up the programme of work; the tables are rearranged and decorated with tins of newly sharpened coloured pencils; the shelf above the radiator is covered with neat piles of exercise books; and one of the window ledges acts as a retrieval point for pencils, rubbers and rulers. Finally, a box of straws and a crate of milk bottles act as a visual reminder that another schoolday is about to begin. . . .

Although the label 'open-plan' is used to describe Mrs Barber's teaching area, the links between the educational and architectural usage of this term are generally weak and implicit. There is little agreement about the theory or practice of open plan schooling. What does it mean? How does it operate? Where did it come from? Where is it going? As a result, teachers and architects remain unable to share their respective understandings and experiences.

Until recently, efforts to overcome this separation of theory and practice have been hindered by the absence of suitable two-way communication channels. Questions posed by practitioners have been obscured or trivialised by the specialist processes and languages of educational research. Not surprisingly, the answers offered by researchers frequently turned out to be inadequate, incomprehensible, or irrelevant.

The essays in this volume are an attempt to reconsider such deficiencies in educational research. They arose from a belief that educational research can gain a great deal from the insights and experiences of educational practitioners—especially those who work in areas of development and innovation. To the extent that schools bear the brunt of educational change, classroom practice is usually more responsive to outside pressures than educational research. For instance, researchers may or may not choose to be fully aware of the educational consequences of changes in the birth rate. Teachers, however, have no such option; they have to adjust to the changes whether they understand them or not. In a more general sense, this places researchers and teachers on opposite sides of the theory/practice divide. Researchers tend to be articulate *about* practice but incompetent *in* practice whereas teachers tend to be competent *in* practice but inarticulate *about* practice. Fortunately, these perspectives are complementary. Thus, this report attempts to merge the skills of researchers and practitioners by making explicit and accessible some of the ideas and practices that have developed alongside the growth of open-plan schooling.

Although they can be read independently or in any order, the essays share a unifying feature. Each one focuses on the emergent rationale or structure of open-plan schooling. In this context the term 'structure' refers to the way in which the separate elements of a school (eg, curriculum, methods, design, administration) can be envisaged—in theory or in practice—as comprising a coherent but dynamic system. Thus the removal of doors and walls does not signal a move towards 'unstructured' education. Rather, it foreshadows a change from one kind of structure to another. Open-plan schools aspire to a logic of their own. They are not ill-assorted aggregates of broken-down classrooms. Their aim is to be different, not degenerate.

Just as the case-study school came to terms with the potentialities of working in an open-plan setting, so these essays try to come to terms with the complexities of contemporary schooling.

The material used in these essays was collected between April 1975 and March 1976. During that time the researcher spent seventy days at the case study school observing the participants at work, interviewing teachers, parents, and children, and writing preliminary reports for submission to the staff. From the outset there was no intention to describe or analyse every aspect of life in an open-plan school. Research topics—selected as the investigation proceeded—were chosen to be of relevance both to the workings of the case-study school and to open-plan schooling in general. As such the essays in this report are more issue-centred than school-centred. They aim to illuminate the general through an analysis of the specific.

The single storey open-plan annexe described in this report was constructed alongside an old classroom building. The original intention was to provide class bases and communal areas for eighteen year-groups of twenty-five children between the ages of five and eight. However, when the new building was opened in September 1974, it also housed some of the primary four (ie, nine-year-old) children. By this time the average size of the primary three and four classes was closer to thirty than twenty-five pupils.

During its first year the annexe was staffed by seventeen class teachers, one full-time gym teacher, two part-time teachers of craft and music and two assistant head teachers (one of whom was also a class teacher). In addition, three full-time auxiliaries assisted the class teachers with their day-to-day work. The routine administration of the open-plan building was shared by the two assistant head teachers who, in turn, liaised with the (male) head teacher of the primary department and the headmaster of the entire school.

The identity of the case-study school has been deliberately omitted from this report. In this analysis of open-plan schooling, its name is not so much a secret as an irrelevance. Similarly, but for different reasons, teachers' and pupils' names have been changed. In so far as all the teachers and pupils in the case-study school were observed, all of them contributed to the research. Hence, to highlight the action or words of one person rather than another is considered to be misleading if not invidious.

The essays in this report fall into three sections. The first section (Chapters 2 and 3) provides some historical context. *Becoming an Open-Plan School* describes the events, controversies and decisions that surrounded the design and inauguration of the case-study building. As such it pinpoints and comments upon some of the broader issues associated with the implementation and management of educational change. The third chapter (*Open-Plan Schools Past and Present*) takes an even wider view and maps out some of the social and educational factors that

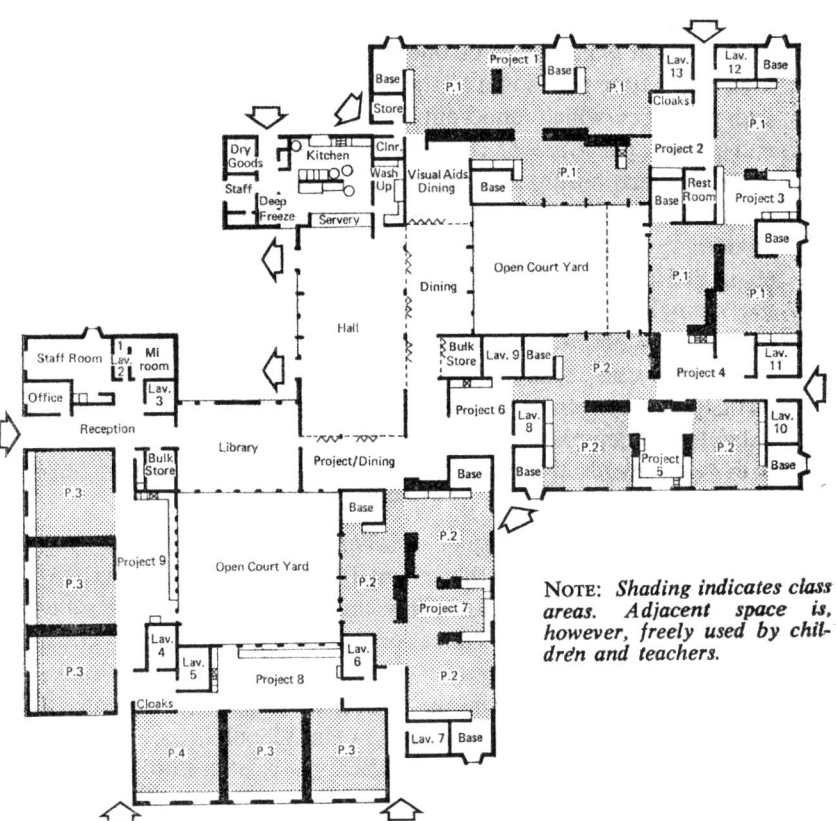

Fig. 1. The case-study building (showing class bases for 1974-75).

have influenced school design over the last three hundred years. Contrary to popular belief, it indicates that classroom-type schools (and class teaching) are also relatively modern forms of educational organisation.

The second section (chapters 4 to 7) probes various aspects of life in an open-plan school. *First Days at School* examines the initial school experiences of one group of five-year-olds. Overall, it attempts to expose some of the invisible strategies, assumptions, and processes which underpin the classroom skills of teachers and pupils. *The Case of the Missing Chairs* (Chapter 5) investigates the relationship between teaching techniques and material resources. Specifically, it questions the widely-held notion that a modern primary school can be organised around less than one chair per pupil. *All Work and no Play?* (Chapter 6) considers the changing character of the primary school curriculum. It concentrates on the problems that confronted a group of teachers in the case-study school who wanted to abolish the conventional distinction between work and play. *Episodes of School Life* (Chapter 7) complements *First Days at School*. It uses material gathered towards the end of the school year and provides day-long accounts of the work of a pupil, a teacher, and a class.

The final section (Chapter 8: *The Logic of the Open-Plan School*) gathers together the salient ideas of the earlier sections. Its purpose is two-fold. First it identifies and interrelates some of the historical events, educational assumptions, and practical constraints that, taken together, have created the form of educational organisation known as open-plan schooling. Second, it underlines the fact that any open-plan school is not a static entity but a finely-balanced, changing, relationship between sets of beliefs and practices. As such, open-plan schooling is always changing in response to new events, new experiences and new ideas.

Thus, the last essay attempts simply to explain the emergence of open-plan schooling, not to justify it in any particular form. Whether or not open-plan schools are a 'good thing' is something that research cannot demonstrate by itself. To the extent that goodness is also related to varying moral and social standards, it cannot be unambiguously deduced from the application of a research technology. Ultimately, the value of open-plan schooling is a matter for the community to decide, not the researcher. The essays in this report may aid that decision making; they cannot replace it.

2

BECOMING AN OPEN-PLAN SCHOOL

> *"Of course every social anthropologist recognises that societies exist within a material context . . . But such context is not simply a passive backcloth to social life; the context itself is a social product and is itself 'structured'."*
>
> (Edmund Leach, *Anthropologist*.)[1]

This essay distils the precipitating events, recurrent issues, and critical decisions that helped to shape the architecture and organisation of the case-study school.

The official and semi-official literature on open-plan schools makes constant reference to the problems faced by teachers moving into new school settings. For example, the report of a DES survey in 1971-72 included the following recommendation:

> "Teachers (particularly but not only head teachers) who are to be transferred to new buildings should have the opportunity to visit schools of similar design and, if possible, their own new school before it is occupied, so that they may more readily prepare for the change."[2]

Similarly, a 1972 EIS report *The Open-Plan Primary School*[3] suggested that 'whenever possible *ad hoc* in-service training

---

[1] Edmund Leach, *Pul Eliya* (Cambridge University Press, 1961), p 306.
[2] Department of Education and Science, *Open-Plan Primary Schools* (London: HMSO, 1972).
[3] Educational Institute of Scotland, *The Open-Plan Primary School* (Edinburgh: EIS, 1972).

courses should be made available to teachers on appointment to open-plan schools' and that 'Colleges of Education should prepare students . . . for employment in open-plan schools' by using the 'expertise and knowledge of teachers experienced in such schools'.

This expressed concern about the novelty of open-plan schooling became a topic for part of this research. It was decided to capitalise upon the 'expertise and knowledge of teachers' by collecting and reporting the experiences of those who had participated in the changeover from the old to the new buildings. Thus, this account not only documents a sequence of events but also presents the participants' views on the significance and value of the change strategies that were followed.

In the Beginning

The origins of the open-plan annexe can be traced back to 1967 when a decision was taken to amalgamate two all-through, grant-aided[4], single sex schools. Although these two schools shared a common name and origin, their main buildings occupied three sites more than a mile from each other. The initial idea— subsequently realised— was for the two separate parts of the girls' school to be transferred to the more extensive boys' campus. At that time, the respective school staffs had very little contact with each other. In particular, the members of the primary departments had evolved different schemes of work and patterns of organisation.

Given the facts that overall pupil numbers were to remain constant before and after the merger, the provision of new buildings on the boys' campus was an immediate concern. A working party was convened by the head teachers of the boys' and girls' schools to explore these and related issues. However, until higher-level decisions had been taken as to the extent, nature, location and financing of the new accommodation, much of the early school-based discussion was couched in very general terms. After some preliminary discussions, the working party discon-

---
[4] Grant-aided schools receive part of their running costs from a central government grant. The remainder are met from charitable sources and/or tuition fees. Approximately 1% of Scottish primary schoolchildren attend grant-aided schools.

tinued its meetings. As one head teacher member pointed out, its continued progress was impeded by a 'lack of something to bite on'.

In 1971, decisions began to crystallise. The primary staffs were officially informed of the development plans. These included the modification of the existing primary building (built in the 1930s) and the construction of a CLASP⁵ open-plan annexe for the younger children. A nine person 'Briefing Panel' was set up to retain overall planning responsibility. Its membership comprised the two infants' mistresses, five other class teachers, the head of the boys' primary department, and, as chairman, the headmistress of the girls' school. The Briefing Panel met formally on seven occasions between June and December 1971. Its work encompassed two broad areas: (1) the preparation of a detailed remit for the architects; and (2) the formulation of organisational plans and educational policy for the new buildings.

By the summer of 1971 the Briefing Panel agreed that the new 'lower primary' accommodation should follow a 'single storey honeycomb plan' and that it should provide teaching bases and communal areas for eighteen groups of twenty-five children (ie, six groups for each year from Primary One to Primary Three). This last decision revised an earlier decision by the head teachers' working party that the new building should provide for the first *four* years of the primary department.

Although the Briefing Panel accepted the prior decision to 'go open-plan', its members shared considerable uncertainty about the educational practicalities of such an innovation. Indeed, the absence of detailed plans at this stage merely heightened the feelings of doubt: the (ill-founded) prospect of a 'hangar' for a school provoked 'strong reactions of horror' among the rest of the staff. To confront these feelings, the architects and the head teachers of the two schools made contact with the CLASP headquarters in Nottinghamshire and, as a consequence, were invited to visit a new open-plan CLASP school in the same county.

---

⁵ (a) This type of school design was initiated by a consortium of local authorities in the East Midlands of England for areas trouble by mining subsidence.
(b) The shell of the case-study school—a CLASP Mark V design—consists of prefabricated units bolted to a steel frame 'floating' on concrete.

Later, the two infants' mistresses and two other class teachers made a similar trip. In the event, this Anglo-Scottish contact proved a turning point. The opportunity to meet other practitioners and to witness a similar open-plan school in operation enabled these senior teachers not only to overcome their own doubts but, equally important, to answer the practical questions posed by their more apprehensive colleagues.

Early Plans

The first sketch plans for the new building were produced in October 1971 and represented an architectural interpretation of the early proposals put forward by the Briefing Panel. Subsequent drawings (see figure 2.1) gradually expressed a more educational emphasis as members of the Panel came to appreciate the limitations and possibilities allowed by the CLASP system. In particular, close attention was paid to the disposition and orientation of the various elements of the plan. For instance the Briefing Panel considered the location of the pupil lavatories (*Were they within easy reach of the teaching areas as well as the playground?*); the size of the class areas (*Could they be expanded by decreasing the size of the home bases?*); the availability of storage space (*What was the optimum balance between centralised and class-based facilities?*); and the extent of the hall (*Could it be realigned or expanded to incorporate one of the adjacent project areas?*).

A series of outside visits also began during this period. By the time the building was eventually occupied, only three teachers (out of twenty) had not been inside another open-plan school. (Most of them had been on official visits, some had made private arrangements, and a few had attended open-plan schools as part of their teacher training.) These outside visits were sometimes reciprocated. The headmistress of the Nottinghamshire CLASP school also spent a planning weekend in Scotland.

The most complex questions discussed by the Briefing Panel arose from the second of its tasks: the formulation of educational policy. In essence, the debates reverberated around two questions: (1) *Should the new building incorporate dining facilities?* (This would mean that the lower primary timetable could include a lunch break and extend beyond one p.m.) (2) *Should the open-plan classes be formed on the basis of year groupings (as used by the boys' school) or should they follow the pattern of the girls' school and include children from more than one annual intake?*

Although these questions appear to be matters of administration, they generated strong and well-remembered disagreements. The minutes of one of the panel meetings faithfully recorded the tone and substance of the debates: 'Views were widely divergent on the desirability of extending the school day beyond the dinner interval and also on the allied questions of open-plan and vertical streaming'. These differences of opinion related not only to pre-existing patterns of organisation but also to contrasting educational philosophies. The representatives of the girls' school hoped to retain the educational continuity of vertical streaming[6], while the teachers from the boys' school saw the introduction of a lunch period as a means of dividing the school day into smaller units of time. Neither side was willing to concede that their ideas were educationally less significant than those of the opposition. To the extent that Panel members aligned themselves on the basis of their existing school allegiances the debates also became as much about 'them' and 'us' as they had been about different patterns and priorities for primary education.

Various alternative solutions were debated at length but a satisfactory compromise successfully eluded the panel. In the meantime, an outside decision to feed older children in the new building meant that dining facilities were, in fact, incorporated in the plans. Nevertheless, the original points of contention still remained at stake. Gradually, it became clear that, taken individually, the issues could not be resolved through compromise; there were no halfway positions that could be adopted.

In this atmosphere of impasse an appeal was made to a higher authority within the school. Following joint discussions between the chairman of the Briefing Panel and the headmaster of the Boys' school (who was also head-designate of the combined schools), the debate was foreclosed in favour of a 'temporary'

---

[6] Alternatively known as vertical grouping or family grouping; vertical streaming involves placing in each teaching unit children whose ages differ by more than one year.

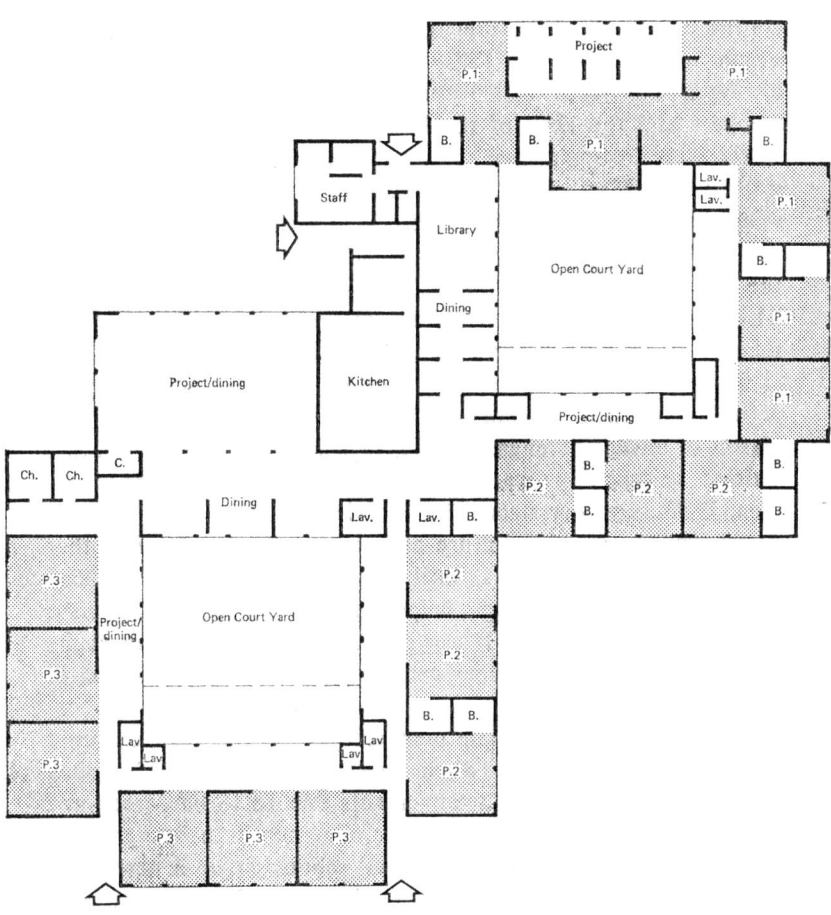

Fig. 2. The case-study building (earliest published plans, 1972).

solution. It was decided that the new open-plan building should follow a system of year grouping (as preferred by the boys' school) while, at the same time, retaining a shortened day for the children in primary one and two (as preferred by the girls' school).

Taking Shape

The following eighteen months were relatively uneventful. The Briefing Panel was disbanded and the architects, surveyors and contractors were left to prepare for the construction phase that began in the summer of 1973. Over this period the school-based arrangements were handled informally by the two assistant head teachers and the head of the boys' primary department—all of whom were to retain their responsibilities when the new building was opened. Most of their joint attention was focussed upon the selection of equipment, furniture and fittings.

The most crucial planning decision at this time hinged upon the optimum allocation of tables and chairs for each class area. This last issue arose in the context of a wider debate. There is a school of thought in primary education—discussed further in chapter four—which holds that a class of children does not need a full complement of chairs and tables since a proportion of the class will always be engaged on non-sitting activities or working outside the teaching area. Whatever the educational merits of this idea, it offers a very strong financial inducement: money that is saved from a global furniture allowance can be spent on other items (eg, storage trolleys, work benches, display screens). The power of this financial logic helped to tip the balance of opinion in the case-study school. It was decided to order sufficient chairs and tables for only sixty per cent of the expected population of the new building.

As the amalgamation date inexorably approached, a new sense of urgency entered the discussions about the new building. Small-scale but essential arrangements needed to be agreed and implemented. In February 1974 (ie, six months before amalgamation) the headmaster of the boys' school set up a new lower primary Working Party which remained in existence until May 1975. This eight-person committee was an extended version of the informal triumvirate which had existed up to that time.

The agenda of the Working Party's first meeting indicates the range of tasks that still remained to be considered:
(1) *Building:* telephones; fire alarm; bells; furniture; blinds/ curtains; clocks.
(2) *Organisation:* allocation of staff, pupils and bases; names of classes; rules and regulations; fire drill; requisition; stock and stationery; textbooks, timetable; specialist staff; intervals; use of hall/dining room; library (use of supervision); plans for removal; remedial work; auxiliaries; care of fabric; access for pupils; communication with parents re opening; curriculum planning; coordination of work; supervision of lunch and play time; organisation of display areas; pianos.
(3) *Running of Department:* assemblies; communication with staff and parents; registers; attendance sheets; reports; confidential records; care and charge of equipment (TV, tape-recorder, radios, record players etc); use of building outwith school hours.

At a later stage the Working Party also outlined the general and specific responsibilities of the three non-teaching auxiliaries (eg, supervision of the playground, recording of radio programmes, preparation of paper and paints); and organised a timetable to suit the specialist teachers (music, craft, remedial and gym), some of whom taught elsewhere.

The only new plans prepared by the lower primary Working Party related to the landscaped play areas that were to adjoin the new building. Again, the discussions were influenced by both economic and educational considerations. Although the Working Party was committed to the idea of specially equipped areas (as had been the case in the girls' school), it was never able to move beyond the stage of preparing sketches and models. Any detailed specifications and estimates had to be put aside until the final (actual) costs of the building became known.

Moving In

At the end of June 1974 all the lower primary teachers at both schools packed their books, materials, and equipment in preparation for the start of term on 20th August. In early August, however, the opening day of the autumn term had to be put back a fortnight since it became clear that the new building would not be ready as planned. Some of the teachers did not learn of this new development until they returned for a staff meeting in the week preceding the 20th August. By then, the entry date required further revision.

These new developments prompted a significant rethink of the plans—it became impossible to delay the start of term any further. Temporary teaching arrangements were brought into operation. Fortunately, the building used previously by the lower primary department of the girls' school was to remain empty until the first of October. It was hastily reopened and used as short-term accommodation for the six primary two classes. The primary three children were not so lucky. The teachers drew lots and moved with their classes into the vacant spaces in the boys' school. The gymnasium, the medical room, and a cloakroom were pressed into service. Meanwhile, the primary one children remained at home for a further three weeks.

Although these bridging solutions undermined the Working Party's plans for a smooth phased entry into the new building, their effects were not entirely negative. For instance, the period of temporary accommodation in the old building gave the primary two children and their teachers a chance to establish working relationships without being faced with the uncertainties of an entirely new situation.

A further consequence of the delays was that much of the teaching apparatus (eg, books and equipment) remained packed away and relatively inaccessible. For this reason the programme of work followed by the teachers during these early weeks necessarily stressed activities that required a minimum of additional materials. This enforced shortage of resources—together with the limitations on space—prompted the teachers to place particular emphasis upon seatwork, especially maths and writing. Later, several of them remarked that in this way their classes had been given a 'flying start' in crucial areas of the curriculum.

A final positive spin-off from the late start to the year was that the individual primary one teachers were better prepared (both mentally and materially) to receive their new classes. While the children were at home (or nursery school) their teachers prepared work cards, organised maths and reading material, and generally thought out what they were going to do when the new building was finally ready. One teacher felt that this made it easier for the children to settle in. Two other teachers also indicated that the advance planning had had more long-term repercussions. Ten months later (ie, when they were interviewed) they attributed the fact that they were 'ahead' in their work to the extra preparation that had been possible the previous September. Finally, one experienced teacher even suggested that the start of the new year had been made easier because the new children were five weeks older.

Eventually, the parents of primary one children were informed that the new building would be open on Monday, 23rd September. Throughout the previous weekend the builders and teachers worked together to render the new annexe habitable. As the carpet was laid, so the tables and chairs were put in position. One week later the primary two classes transferred from the girls' school and the primary three classes crossed the playground from the old building as their individual areas were made ready. As indicated in figure 1.1, the classes were clustered together. Each year-cohort occupied a different part of the building.

By the middle of October 1974 the new building had become the sole workplace for twenty teachers, three auxiliaries, seven cleaners, five kitchen staff, and about 470 children.

Contrary to expectation ('We prepared for a disaster that never happened') the transfer proved relatively uneventful. No major difficulties interrupted the 'smooth chaos' of the actual move: 'The children didn't turn a hair . . . They came in and sat down and we never looked back'. The only contrary reports came from the three teachers who were new to the staff; and from the primary one teachers whose class areas were flooded by a burst pipe shortly after the start of term.

First Reactions

Because of the long period leading up to the establishment of the new building, seventy-five per cent of the teachers had at least two years' warning of the move. The remaining staff joined the school within that period but, in every case, knew about the open-plan building before accepting their appointments. One benefit of this advance notice was that both contributing schools had already begun to move towards more open-plan forms of organisation. Classroom doors in the old buildings were left open; children were encouraged to move about the school unsupervised; and corridor space was used for quiet areas or for painting, craft and library work. Thus, the children as well as the teachers and parents were encouraged to reflect upon the changes that were imminent.

Even so, the teachers faced the move with mixed feelings. Excitement about the possibilities of such a design were tempered with apprehension about new and possibly intractable difficulties. Maintenance of educational standards, elimination of noise interference, and management of the new building's openness were repeatedly cited in this respect. Latterly, the merger of two separate staffs—each with their own established patterns of precedent and usage—was also envisaged as a potential source of difficulty.

In the event, many of the anticipated problems were much less prominent than expected. The novelty of the open-plan setting, the stop-go atmosphere at the beginning of term, and the urgency surrounding the actual move gave the teachers (and children) only limited opportunity to dwell upon such difficulties. One member of the working party characterised the staff at this period as 'sisters in adversity'. 'We were all waiting to fall off the precipice . . . (but) we jolly well had to get on with it' was the explanation offered by another participant.

Despite a range of teething troubles (eg, repeated failure of the heating system; fire doors that would not shut; windows that would not open; lights that fused whenever the kitchen was in use; and toilet handles that fell off at the slightest hint of juvenile pressure), the rest of the first term passed relatively uneventfully. Although the delivery of furniture and equipment was delayed, most of the critical deficiencies could be rectified using supplies from the old buildings. This proved especially significant with regard to the level of seating. All the teachers—even those who had been in favour of a reduced provision—'topped up' their complement of chairs and, in some cases, raised the level to over one hundred per cent.

The remaining task for the lower primary Working Party during the first year's occupation of the new building was the compilation and recompilation of a 'snagging list' for presentation to the contractors and suppliers. While these shortcomings and deficiencies were gradually overcome, the completion of the outside adventure playground proved impossible. No further funds were forthcoming and the scheme was reluctantly allowed to lapse.

The final organisation of the new building differed from the intended brief in two respects. First, it included one primary four class and second, it embodied an incipient form of vertical streaming. The presence of the primary four class arose from an interim decision to decrease the size of the overall school roll by about 15 per cent over three years. For this reason the new annexe opened with a transitional form of organisation: eighteen classes spread over four years in the ratio 6: 6: 5: 1. The start of the 1975 autumn term saw a further contraction (5: 5: 5: 3). The 1976-7 complement of the open-plan annexe was five groups of twenty-five children in primary one and two, and four groups of thirty in primary three and four.

The gradual emergence of a weak form of vertical streaming also accompanied the decrease in school role. In the resultant re-shuffle two teachers did not move from their original teaching areas when they took new classes in 1975-6. As a result children in primary two, three and four began to work in areas originally designed for younger children. More important, they began to work alongside these children in the communal areas.

Ironically, both of these changes took the school back towards forms of organisation that, after much deliberation, the 1971 Briefing Panel had decided to reject.

IN RETROSPECT

This account began by quoting the reports of two surveys, both of which implied that in recent years very few teachers have had the opportunity to 'readily prepare' for any move into a newly-designed school building. If this state of affairs is still true, then the events described above must be considered exceptional. They are, however, in line with what the reports indicate to be desirable. For this reason, if no other, they are worthy of further comment.

1. Many interpretations of educational change focus on the short-term difficulties and constraints. By placing events in a more extensive time-span, this account suggests that the move into a new building was only a minor episode in a series of long term and perhaps more momentous changes. The earlier decisions to integrate two single sex schools, to implement vertical streaming and to open classroom doors may, in fact, have represented a much more profound reorientation of the schools' educational values.

2. Although published accounts typically stress the importance of consultation between architects and teachers, they focus very little attention upon the attendant problems. The guiding assumption is that teachers know what they want; that they can agree about it among themselves; and that they can articulate their requirements in architectural terms. As this account indicates, none of these conditions is easily fulfilled. In particular, the design sequence used by educationalists may not fit the conventions of architectural and building practice. For example, decisions that teachers would perhaps regard as relatively low down on their list of priorities may, in fact, be pre-empted by earlier and irreversible decisions unwittingly taken by architects.

3. Similarly, prior discussions need not always produce consensus. There is always the possibility that they will generate heat rather than light. More important, differences of opinion may, as shown above, prove to be logically irreconcileable.

4. There is a further architectural issue which relates to the difference between building an entirely new school and building an extension or replacement for an existing school. When a new school is commissioned, many of the major decisions will, almost inevitably, have been taken before the appointment of staff. Thus the main problem is administrative—choosing the staff to fit the new building. When, however, an extension is to be built, the

main problem is in the realm of design—fitting the school to the (existing) staff.

5. Advance educational planning is a precarious and delicate affair. Although it is possible to make elaborate preparations for a move into a new building, such plans can never cover all eventualities. Overplanning may create more difficulties than it solves. Indeed, the most crucial planning decisions may be the identification of those issues which are to be deliberately neglected.

6. While a single unrepeatable event like a coronation or moonshot must be planned and rehearsed to the utmost detail, the opening of a school is a rather different affair. In an educational sense it is very difficult, if not arbitrary, to stipulate the point at which a school has become fully operational since cumulated experiences offer fresh opportunities and changed circumstances bring new problems.

7. The admittance of the outside visitors to a new school poses special problems. It is sometimes suggested—as in the DES report —that new schools should be free from outside visitors. Yet, at the same time, it is also proposed that teachers should be encouraged to visit other 'schools of a similar design'. If comparable schools are built and opened at about the same time, then both these conditions cannot be fulfilled simultaneously.

8. Although the logical analysis of the previous paragraph may seem rather academic, it has real practical consequences. For instance, what policy should a new school adopt when faced with requests from prospective visitors? Should it impose a twelve-month moratorium and anxiously prepare for a 'gala' opening? Or should it allow spectators to attend its early and possibly fumbling rehearsals? Clearly, there are a number of considerations which might influence such a decision. First, any new school cannot impose a strict ban on visitors. A constant succession of adults will almost certainly pass through the building while classes are at work—tradesmen, architects, commercial representatives, administrators, inspectors (fire as well as educational) and so on. Second, visitors can be regarded as a resource as well as a hindrance. In certain circumstances an exchange of views with outsiders may help insiders to clarify

their ideas or, better still, to resolve their immediate problems. Third, a policy with regard to visitors will also be influenced by the context of the school. It will depend, for example, on the status of the visitors, on the locality of the school (it is almost impossible to 'drop in' on a remote school); on the size of the visiting party; on the pattern and frequency of previous visits; on the type of activities that take place within the school; and, not least, on the collective predispositions of the receiving teachers. In certain schools it may be possible to treat visitors as a natural and unexceptional part of the school day whereas in other settings their presence would be surrounded with the trappings of a formal ceremony.

Summary

This essay has attempted to present the precipitating events and critical decisions that helped to shape the environment of one particular new school. Much more could be written. Nevertheless, to the extent that this account is concise rather than encyclopaedic it may provide an accessible starting point and some well-marked signposts for other people contemplating a similar journey. While it is true, of course, that other travellers will have different destinations, it is also true that many of them will use equivalent means of transport.

3

OPEN-PLAN SCHOOLS PAST AND PRESENT

> "Structure itself occurs in the process of becoming . . . it takes shape and breaks down ceaselessly."
>
> (Emile Durkheim, *Sociologist*.)[1]

Originally, this essay was planned as a descriptive account of changes in primary school design in Scotland since the 1940s. Further research, however, drew attention to a nineteenth century variant of the open-plan idea known as the monitorial system. Almost by chance, these inquiries revealed that the case-study school had also introduced a monitorial form of organisation in that period. Thus, there is a sense in which, for the second time in its history, the case-study school has 'gone open-plan'.

A popular explanation for the emergence of open-plan schools in Scotland is that they are cheaper to build than comparable 'classroom' schools. A more sophisticated argument is that open-plan schools represent a tacit (if not malign) conspiracy between cost-conscious administrators, award-seeking builders and architects, and progressive (ie, non-teaching) educationalists.

In a narrow sense these ideas are correct. Yet, viewed historically, they lose much of their logical force. They may account for the establishment of open-plan schools but, equally, they can be used to explain every other change in school design since before the Reformation. Although such analyses can suggest

---

[1] Quoted in C Levi-Strauss, *The Scope of Anthropology* (London: Jonathan Cape, 1967), pp 29-30.

the sources of motive power in the education system, they are unable to predict the actual form the system will take. To explain patterns of school practice and design in economic or administrative terms is rather like predicting the destination of a travelling motor car simply from a knowledge of its engine size.

Thus, to provide a more specific account of open-plan schools it is necessary to consider a much wider range of influences and events. This brief essay attempts such a task. It tries to distinguish and unravel some of the social, religious, political, economic, demographic and educational factors that have helped to shape Scotland's elementary and primary schools in the past and in the present.

The first section (*After the Reformation*) discusses the parochial school system that spread through Scotland in the seventeenth and eighteenth century; the second part (*The Industrial Revolution*) indicates the changes that led to the introduction of a form of open-plan schooling in the early part of the nineteenth century; the final section (*Open-plan Revisited*) outlines the events that foreshadowed the reintroduction of a comparable school design after the Second World War.

AFTER THE REFORMATION

The basis for a national system of schooling in Scotland dates from the Reformation. In the religious and political ferment of that time, formal moral education was proposed as a means of repairing and revitalising the torn fabric of a disordered society. The *First Book of Discipline,* a policy document prepared by John Knox and others in 1560, advocated that rudimentary instruction in the principles of religion should be offered, without regard to sex or class, to the youth of the nation. Nearly 150 years elapsed before this revolutionary vision of universal schooling finally obtained the force of law: in 1696 the *Act for Settling of Schools* laid down that local landowners (ie, taxpayers) were to provide sufficient funds for a schoolmaster and schoolhouse in each parish.

To some extent this Act brought the law into line with existing practice. Certain parishes already provided schooling on the basis of permissive legislation; and many towns continued to support burgh schools founded before the Reformation.

Prior to the establishment of day schools, children of the 'lower orders' received their only formal instruction through the agency of the church. The minister or his assistant (usually known as a 'reader' or 'catechist') took extra Sunday services which were designed to extend and reinforce the teachings of the church. Families with additional material resources were able to make a more elaborate provision. Tutors could be employed in the home; and older boys could be sent away to College (ie, University) or to one of the more prestigious burgh schools (eg, Edinburgh High School). For most young people, however, secular or vocational education remained an informal process—the responsibility of their parents or employers (often the same people).

As decreed by the Act of 1696, most parishes retained only one teacher and one school. The schoolroom usually formed part of the 'commodious' dwelling provided for the schoolmaster. If not, the church, the home of one of the pupils, or some other building served as a substitute.

Not surprisingly, the schoolhouses and schoolrooms of the eighteenth century were small and sparsely furnished. Here is how one historian has described the schoolhouses of that period:

> Built in accordance with local custom, they were simple cottages, sometimes of one apartment, sometimes a 'but and ben'—structures of dry stonework, with two small windows and a rough deal door. The inner walls were clarted or smeared with a mixture of clay and cowdung. The roof of undressed rafters and cross spars supported a thatching of fern, heather, or straw. . . . The floor was of trodden earth or clay. The single cottage was divided by a wooden partition, thus forming living quarters for the master at one end and accommodation for the school at the other.[2]

The inside dimensions of the house were as small as ten metres by four metres and the only furniture in the schoolroom was likely to be the seating offered by tree trunks or rough-hewn

[2] J. Mason, "Scottish charity schools of the eighteenth century", *Scottish Historical Review*, Vol 33, (1954), p 4.

planks. (The use of tables, desks, slates and blackboards did not become widespread until the middle of the nineteenth century.)

Guided by the wisdom of the national church, the local presbyteries drew up rules and regulations for the parish schools that fell within their jurisdiction. The school timetable was similar to that of the collegiate (ie, monastic) schools of the pre-Reformation period. The school day lasted from dawn to dusk and was divided into two or three sessions with at least an hour in between. Schools were open for five and a half to six days per week and only closed for about two weeks at Christmas and five weeks in the summer.

The teaching methods used in the parochial schools also followed the ancient ecclesiastical model. The 'lesson' was read out line by line and the school children responded individually or in unison. By these non-literate means, children began to learn the Lord's Prayer, the Creed, and the more popular psalms.

The most significant educational changes in the post-Reformation period came in the realm of curriculum. School texts had to meet the approval of the newly established church. In 1648, for example, the Church of Scotland produced its own version of the Shorter Catechism to replace a privately produced edition which was felt to be theologically suspect. This early textbook contained simple questions and answers of a religious or moral character which schoolchildren were expected to learn by heart (eg, Who created you? Answer: God; Of what was (sic) you made? Answer: Of the dust of the earth.)

Clearly, much of what passed for instruction in an eighteenth century school was repetitious; the form and content of the basic lessons varied little from day to day. Nevertheless, children who achieved proficiency were given a chance to demonstrate their virtue by leading the catechism. Any child who filled this role regularly became known as the *dux* (ie, leader) of the class—a term still used in Scottish schools to describe the most academically successful pupil.

The Shorter Catechism also played its part as a reading primer. From 1696 it appeared with individual letters (and numbers) printed on the cover and was widely used in that form until the end of the nineteenth century. Later editions also included syllables. Children who had learned their 'letters' graduated to the more complex syllabic sounds and then on to the printed material inside the Catechism. Gradually, therefore, children began to learn from print rather than through the medium of verbal communication. Not until the middle of the nineteenth century did the first 'R' finally take its place as a basic element in the school curriculum.

For many children this type of rudimentary instruction represented the high point of their formal schooling. Any additional subjects required special equipment (books, papers and pens) and the payment of supplementary fees to the schoolmaster. For these reasons, if no others, writing and arithmetic remained educational luxuries.

Throughout this period, parental poverty, outbreaks of famine, epidemics of disease, the seasonal demands of an agricultural economy, and the reluctance of landowners to pay higher taxes all helped to keep school attendance and pupil achievement at a low level. There is still some doubt whether every parish could claim the existence of a regularly functioning school or, indeed, whether the related precept of universal education was widely accepted among the tax-paying sections of the community.

In the context of this account, however, it is perhaps more important to consider what happened to the children who actually went to school than to argue about the overall levels of schooling. It would be interesting, for example, to establish the varying patterns of school attendance. (Did the pupils attend all day and every day? What happened during the summer when they were required to work on the land?) Likewise, historians know relatively little about the composition, size, and work of the schools. (What age range did they cater for? What was the ratio of boys to girls? Did adults attend in the winter? Did whole class teaching methods predominate? Did the curriculum vary for different children?)

The evidence relating to all these questions is, as yet, rather fragmentary. Different sources yield different estimates. It is not clear, for example, whether every child was expected to attend all of the day-time sessions prescribed by the presbyteries. It is certainly true, however, that extra (ie, specialist) classes were held in the early morning or evening, but it is much less clear how the intervening periods were spent.

The regulation curricula of the eighteenth century are somewhat better understood. An indication of their form and content can be learned from presbytery records. Certain parish schools —like most of the burgh schools—offered advanced courses which were taken (and paid for) subject by subject. Besides reading and writing, the older and more successful boys might receive instruction in Latin (essential for university in the early eighteenth century); geography (biblical and modern); arithmetic (actually a form of book-keeping); navigation and French. Such a curriculum did not emerge by chance. The gradual spread of these secular subjects accurately reflected Scotland's growing status as a trading nation.

THE INDUSTRIAL REVOLUTION

From the middle of the eighteenth century the type of schooling described above began to change. The industrial revolution, an unprecedented growth in population (65% between 1755 and 1820), and migration towards the growing industrial centres all helped to place the parochial school system under increasing pressure.

Within the existing framework of legislation, the lowland schools were unable to cope: the law only stipulated that one school and one schoolmaster could be maintained by local taxation. In short, an education system devised in the sixteenth century to meet the small-scale needs of Scotland's domestic and rural economy could no longer satisfy the growing technological appetite of the factory system nor act as an effective guardian of the nation's morals.

The school system began to diversify as different localities, groups and individuals sought to fill the gap between the increased demands and the limited supply. A wide range of non-parochial institutions began to flourish. 'Adventure' schools were set up by private teachers; 'subscription' schools were founded by groups who then employed a teacher; charitable schools were established by organisations like the Society in Scotland for the

Propagation of Christian Knowledge; the church 'sessional' schools were formed to augment the existing parochial provision.

Despite these efforts, the number of children who were bypassed by the school system continued to be a source of national alarm. Most of the recommended solutions were based on the provision of extra one-teacher schools. Schemes of this type were woefully inadequate. They were not only undermined by a shortage of suitable teachers but also by the inability of many of their prospective pupils to pay for such an education—even if it could be provided. The problem, therefore, was both economic and educational.

An alternative solution—to increase the pupil/teacher ratio—was rarely considered. Certain burgh schools had large classes (eg, 150 boys) but also employed specialist tutors (eg, for English, writing, Latin) who worked alongside the master. Such forms of organisation however, presupposed a wealthy population which could provide the necessary accommodation and salaries.

By 1810, however, a radically new form of school organisation —the monitorial system—began to gain ground in the urban areas of Scotland. Basically, it offered a solution to the problems of mass education. Some years previously, the Rev Dr Andrew Bell (a Church of England minister born in St Andrews) had been made superintendent of a military male asylum (orphanage) near Madras on the Indian subcontinent. While discharging his duties Bell had devised a system whereby hundreds of pupils could be taught in the same room by one master assisted by monitors drawn from the more able pupils.

As befits its origins, the monitorial system was run on military lines. 'Drilling' was the educational order of the day. Here is a contemporary account of the system as it was used in the 1820s to educate the 600 boys of the Edinburgh sessional school.

> "The tables are placed round the walls of the schoolroom, and the remainder of the floor is left quite unoccupied by furniture, except for the master's desk. One half of the scholars always sit at the desks with their faces to the wall, employed in learning to write or cypher, while the other half stand on the floor, either reading, or practising the rules of arithmetic. The classes on the floor are ranged in segments of circles behind each other, fronting the

master's desk, which is at the head of the room and, in front of each class, are placed the teaching monitor and his assistant, whose duty it is to preserve order and attention.

At five minutes before ten every morning (except Sunday) the school bell is rung. Every boy enters with his slate slung around his neck. Precisely on the stroke of ten on the school clock the doors are closed for prayer, which is offered up by the master. That duty having been performed, the words of command are successively given, 'recover slates', 'sling slates', 'recover books', 'give pencils', 'second division, seats'. The classes of the elder division then proceed to read, spell, explain, or learn grammar etc under their respective monitors, while the children of the second division write or cypher until half past ten. At that time the first division are marched to their seats, and the second division ocupy their places on the floor, a revolution which is performed in about a minute and a half. The second division then proceed to read or spell, and the first to write till eleven o'clock, when another shift takes place. . . ." (Quotation abridged.)[3]

Although Bell and other protagonists claimed the monitorial system as a new 'discovery' (sic), it had certain similarities with the methods already used in the larger burgh schools. Nevertheless, whatever its origins, the open-plan monitorial system was the beginning of cheap urban education in Scotland. Its rationale became widely known in the 1840s through the work of John Gibson, the first Inspector of Schools to be appointed in Scotland and a former master of the Madras Academy in St Andrews.

With the aid of the monitorial system and its many derivatives, the one-teacher school was retained in urban areas. It continued to be the norm until the last quarter of the nineteenth century. Around that time, however, changes in legislation, a growth in the number of qualified teachers, and various innovations in building technique (eg, the development of central heating) made it educationally possible to incorporate a group of one-teacher schools under the same roof. These major developments initiated two trends which have continued to the present day: a gradual increase in school size, and a gradual decrease in the pupil/teacher ratio. (In 1872 the size of the average school receiving

[3] J Wood, *Account of the Edinburgh Sessional School* (Edinburgh: John Wardlaw, 1828).

public grants was 102 pupils, and the pupil/teacher ratio was 80:1. By 1967 the comparable figures were 295 and 22:1.)

The monitorial schools resembled present-day open-plan schools in three respects: (i) they had more than one instructor working in the same schoolroom; (ii) they made very little provision for circulation (ie, corridor) space; and (iii) they not only fitted a particular method of instruction but also resonated with the demands of a limited budget. By the same token, of course, there are many differences between the two systems, particularly in the areas of curriculum and teaching method.

In practice, the monitorial schools of the nineteenth century signalled, if not hastened, the decline of the parochial school system which had served Scotland for more than a century and a half. However, as shown below, the image of the one-teacher rural school has continued to have a formative influence on the organisation and design of elementary and primary schools.

OPEN-PLAN REVISITED

For a number of reasons—largely stemming from a decline in the birth rate and from the general economic malaise—the Scottish education system was relatively quiescent before the Second World War. The war era, however, marked the beginning of a thirty-year period of massive expansion and renewal (eg, 85% of all school places in Scotland are in buildings completed since 1946). Although the need to replace and repair damaged schools was an immediate concern, the overriding pressures for change were social and political rather than economic and technical. The 1940s were pervaded by a visionary atmosphere of social reconstruction. The most obvious educational outcomes of this period were the wartime legislation separating primary and secondary education and the associated decision to raise the school leaving age from 14-15 years (enacted in 1947).

Initial efforts to build new schools and rebuild old ones were hampered by a shortage of skilled labour and a dearth of traditional materials (eg, bricks). These shortcomings prompted the Government to initiate the Hutted Operation for the Raising of the School Leaving Age. A standard rectangular design was worked out which could be constructed with prefabricated components. When these grey, single-storey concrete HORSA huts were erected between 1947 and 1953 they provided accommodation for nearly 200,000 British schoolchildren (separate Scottish figures are not available). As a result the raising of the school leaving age was carried out successfully. According to official reports, no children had their schooling curtailed for lack of accommodation.

The HORSA scheme for the design and erection of schools was so successful that in the late 1940s the Ministry of Education in London established a Development Group—headed jointly by an HMI and an architect—to assist local authorities with their own post-war school building programmes. Although the HORSA huts relieved the pressure on secondary schools caused by the raising of the school leaving age, a new pressure was being created by an increase in the birth rate and an associated movement of (mainly) young families towards the towns.

The HMI in charge of the Development Group was Derek Morrell—later to become a formative figure in the early years of the Schools Council. To create schools which could accommodate the new ideas in primary education, Morrell presented his architectural colleagues with an educational brief based on certain strong assumptions about the utilisation of space:

> "Post-war schools need more useful floor area than those built before World War Two. . . . (They) need more individual spaces . . . of many different sizes and shapes. . . . Some of the spaces will be quiet and clean, others noisy and dirty. The tools to be used may be pens, needles, chisels, lathes, pianos or vaulting horses. There is thus a need for very different physical conditions in different spaces. These spaces must be adaptable not only to present variety of uses; but also to the changes which the future is bound to bring, sometimes suddenly, sometimes imperceptibly. The spaces are designed for children."[4]

In turn, the architects responded with a set of solutions that

---

[4] D H Morrell and A Pott, *Britain's New Schools* (London: Longmans, 1960).

could be accommodated within the official scheme of cost limits (introduced in 1950). System building, multiple use of space and compactness of design were the key features. By such means the amount of designated teaching space per child was increased between the 1940s and the 1960s while, at the same time, the ratio of construction costs to teaching space was actually lowered. Although, as indicated, architects and educationalists had a very strong impact on school design, their influence upon practice was probably less pronounced. The changes in curriculum and methods that occurred over the same period affected all schools. Two important catalysts were the gradual withdrawal of secondary school selection and the slow but steady decrease in class sizes.

The success of the Ministry of Education Development Group prompted certain local authorities to create their own building consortia. In 1957, for example, Nottinghamshire County Council initiated the Consortium of Local Authorities Special Programme (CLASP) to tackle the specific problems associated with building schools in areas troubled by mining subsidence.

Meanwhile, the Development Group began to integrate the knowledge it had gained in rural and semi-rural areas like Hertfordshire and Oxfordshire. Particular attention was focused on the relative disposition of space within a school, on the distribution of resources which could be shared, and on the utilisation of unused areas inside and around the building. In turn, there was a blurring of the architectural and educational boundaries that had previously separated indoors from outdoors, corridors from cloakrooms, and classrooms from halls and dining rooms. Later, when the first designated open-plan school was built in 1959 for fifty pupils at Finmere in Oxfordshire, some of these physical boundaries were removed entirely.

The introduction of open-plan ideas into rural schools was relatively easy. Many of the 'new' methods advocated at that time (eg, mixed-ability teaching, vertical streaming) had always been an inevitable part of their stock in trade. In this educational sense, therefore, small rural schools have never ceased to be open-plan.

After the experience of working on small schools, the Development Group felt ready to tackle a larger urban setting. Working with the Plowden Committee, the Eveline Lowe primary school was designed in 1963 to accommodate 320 inner-London children. From that time, open-plan schools became predominantly a suburban phenomenon. They were built on new housing estates to cope with localised fluctuations in the numbers of children of primary age.

The above information about the post-war development of primary school design is derived solely from the English experience. Partly this is because the comparable Scottish information is not so readily available but partly, too, because many of the centralised initiatives—such as the HORSA scheme and the withdrawal of secondary school selection—applied no less to Scotland than to England and Wales. Nevertheless, in the absence of confirmatory evidence it would be incorrect to assume automatically that identical sets of conditions applied north and south of the border.

Certainly, however, there are a number of similarities. The first post-war Scottish open-plan primary school (Kirkhill, in West Lothian) was opened in 1969, two years after the Eveline Lowe School. Likewise both of these schools were built in conjunction with major government reports on primary education. The Eveline Lowe School was an attempt to give concrete form to the ideas of the *Plowden Report (1967)* and Kirkhill school was designed to illustrate the principles set out in the Scottish Education Department Memorandum *Primary Education in Scotland (1965)*. A further parallel is that Kirkhill—like Eveline Lowe—was also a cooperative venture; this time between the Scottish Education Department and the West Lothian County Council.

More recent developments have also matched the English experience. The major Scottish centres of open-plan schooling—such as Aberdeenshire and the Lothians—have also been located in comparable areas of suburban expansion.

Nevertheless, a range of peculiarly Scottish factors—listed below—have also intervened in the process. Hence, although it is possible to relate school architecture to a set of United Kingdom conditions it is also necessary to cite more local influences if the explanation is to encompass the changes in curriculum and teaching method that emerged over the same period.

1. Between 1964 and 1966 three new colleges of education were opened in Scotland (Hamilton, Craigie and Callendar Park). Each of these institutions were specifically designed to meet the increased needs of primary education. Since that time these colleges have been free to develop specialist teacher training in the areas of primary and infant education without being overshadowed by the assumption of secondary education.

2. This increase (from seven to ten colleges) led directly to an influx of staff. Some new lecturers came from England and were recruited on the basis of their experience in innovatory primary schools. The expansion of the colleges also created a bulge of young teachers fully informed about the educational ideas that were current at that time.

3. In 1965 the SED regulations for the training of teachers were changed. It no longer became possible for a teacher to become certificated for both primary and secondary education. This change was reflected in a decrease in the number of secondary school teachers (and especially male graduates) who were appointed with secondary school ideas to posts as headmasters of primary schools.

4. 1966 saw the first appointment of a Froebel-trained teacher to the post of HMI. The Froebel qualification (now renamed) required additional training in infant and lower primary methods and was increasingly taken by experienced rather than newly qualified teachers. As such, many Froebel students immediately took up influential posts of responsibility when they returned to the school system.

5. In the mid 1960s, education authorities began to appoint Advisers with special responsibility for primary schools. Certain of these Advisers have since been prominent in the development of open-plan schools.

6. Over the same period there has also been a growth of in-service training (ie, retraining) for teachers. This, too, has helped in the dissemination of ideas.

7. Likewise, there has been a greater degree of job mobility

among teachers. Again, this has increased the possibility that innovatory practices might spread from school to school.

8. Finally, the growth of pre-schooling in the late 1960s and early 1970s not only brought infant ideas to the attention of more schools and teachers but also to the attention of greater numbers of parents. To some extent this may have facilitated the introduction of open-plan forms of organisation (used for many years in nursery schools) into the early years of the primary school.

Conclusion

This essay has tried to throw light on some of the changes that have occurred in the history of elementary and primary education in Scotland. The overall picture—like the historical record—is inevitably incomplete and uneven. It is difficult, therefore, to weigh the importance of specific events and trends. Nevertheless, this account would indicate that if the birth-rate continues to decline at the present rate, then the construction of new open-plan primary schools in Scotland may, in fact, become a relatively rare occurrence. Instead, new forms of open-plan architecture will probably survive in the secondary sector where they will continue to foster the same educational assumptions (eg, activity methods, curriculum integration, non-class teaching) that were realised many years previously in the infant schoolroom. Whether these 'open-plan' ideas achieve pre-eminence will, as in the past, depend for a large part on the secondary school examination system. This system—currently under review—is a major influence on the curriculum and teaching methods used in Scotland's schools.

Whatever the outcome of this official review it is certain that open-plan schools, like the parochial, monitorial, and classroom systems that preceded them, will continue to influence as well as to reflect the changing fortunes of the nation's life.

Further Reading

To the extent that education is placed in a wider context, the best introduction to the history of Scottish education can be found in T C Smout, *A History of the Scottish People 1560-1830*

(London: Collins, 1969). Similarly, the best general history of early education is N Whitbread, *The Evolution of the Nursery-Infant School 1800-1970* (London: Routledge & Kegan Paul, 1972). A brief but extremely valuable source-book on school design is J McNicholas, *The Design of English Elementary and Primary Schools: a select annotated bibliography* (London: National Foundation for Educational Research, 1974).

4

FIRST DAYS AT SCHOOL

> *"These [observations of classroom life] reveal that what may seem random and unstructured moment-by-moment may have a structure when viewed cumulatively over a period of time."*
>
> (Rob Walker & Clem Adelman, *Educationalists.*)[1]

This essay considers the strategies, assumptions, and processes which underly the more visible aspects of teaching in a primary school. It builds upon the work of one class of five-year-olds and their teacher as observed over a fourteen-day period at the beginning of the autumn term. The first part provides an explanatory commentary of the events of that period. The second part is more speculative. It extends the initial idea and tries to identify some of the 'intangibles' of teaching.

For more than a decade British primary education has been the object of international attention. As a result, certain schools have been inundated by a wave of visiting teachers, administrators, politicians and researchers—some of whom have recorded their impressions for a wider audience.

Obviously, such published accounts differ widely in their scope and quality: some have achieved best-seller status, others, no doubt, have remained unread. All, however, dwell preferentially on the more innovative and visible aspects of school life. Here is an illustration taken from one of the best known examples:

---

[1] R Walker and C Adelman, *A Guide to Classroom Observation* (London: Methuen, 1975), p. 56.

"ITEM: An infant school, also in a rapidly changing immigrant neighbourhood in London. At one side of the hall, a small wooden platform serves as a stage for two splendidly costumed little girls, recent immigrants from the West Indies, who are improvising a ballet for the headmistress. Two more girls, of Cockney origin, join the ballet and soon eight more youngsters sit down to watch, applauding enthusiastically when the ballet ends. While this is going on, three boys are busily engaged in building a castle in one corner, while in another corner a boy and girl, playing the xylophone, are joined by four more. . . ."[2]

Sketch book material such as this provides only part of the story. It gives the impression that the modern primary school is a stable, harmonious system populated by autonomous and mutually supportive individuals. It accurately outlines a set of polished performances, but, in doing so, fails to recall the weeks of repetitious rehearsals, the occasions when the actors forgot their lines, or the nights when the lights failed and the scenery collapsed.

To a degree, this type of foreshortened perspective is inevitable. It arises from the brief duration of the school visits. Thus, to fill in the background a different kind of investigation is required. To understand fully the significance of a classroom event it is not sufficient merely to observe its enactment, it is also necessary to be aware of its history, to be alert to its possible outcomes and, above all, to be sensitive to the thoughts and intentions that guide its participants. In short, it is necessary to move much closer to the day to day world of teachers and pupils.

This essay—which focuses on a class of five-year-olds during their first day at primary school—attempts to make such a shift. That is, it is concerned not only with the turbulent stream of classroom events, but also with the reasons, strategies, patterns, and processes that lie beneath its surface.

The decision to study this age group was based on two related assumptions. First, that a child's attempts to come to terms with the distinctive features of schooling are likely to be more visible at this age that at any other time. And secondly, that the beginning of a new school year is the occasion when experienced

[2] C Silberman, *Crisis in the Classroom: The Remaking of American Education*) (New York: Vintage Books, 1971), pp 224-5.

teachers are usually most explicit about the codes of practice (rules, standards, sanctions, etc) which they use to regulate the social diversity of classroom life.

The core data were gathered on nine of the first fourteen days of the school year. A longhand record was kept of the general flow of classroom events and day by day a typed transcript of these notes was returned to the teacher for her reactions. These initial data were then augmented by interviews with at least one parent of each child and by the observer's experience of teaching the class for two days later in the term.

Thus, the evidence in this account is drawn from the fieldnotes and the parent interviews, whereas the interpretative commentary is derived from a dialogue between the teacher and the observer conducted over the remaining weeks of the term. To simplify the reader's task, the commentary can be read independently of the evidence.

DAY ONE

At 8.20am on Tuesday, 26th August, Mrs Robertson arrives at school for the first day of the autumn term. (It is not only the start of her fifth year of teaching since leaving college, but also the start of her fifth year in the same school.) The class area already shows signs of her presence. Pictures are displayed on the wall; games and maths equipment are laid out on two trestle tables; paper, crayons, and plasticine are arranged on some of the low tables; and the house, library, and painting areas are carefully rendered attractive as well as accessible.

Stephen and his mother arrive while Mrs Robertson is in the staff room. In the meantime, Miss Downie (an assistant Head teacher) takes Stephen under her wing and shows him round the class area. Mrs Robertson returns and takes over from Miss Downie. Michael arrives with his mother and father. Both boys are shown where to put their coats and schoolbags. At Mrs Robertson's prompting, Stephen and Michael choose a game or activity and are shown to one of the small tables. They are left to fend for themselves as more children arrive. While being shown around the area each child is drawn into conversation by Mrs Robertson ('What is your name? What would you like to do?')

Michael gets up from his chair leaving a large wooden shoe (used for learning how to tie laces) on the table. Noticing this, Mrs Robertson shows him how to put it back in its 'proper' place (ie, on the high table). Meanwhile Nicola is rolling the plasticine on a table instead of on a board. Like Michael she is shown how to follow the correct procedure.

At 8.50am the last few children are waiting to be taken round the class area. By nine o'clock all the children who are due to come on the first day have arrived. Three are sitting at the plasticine table; two are working with jigsaws; one is assembling unifix (maths) blocks; and three are just watching. The children begin to talk among themselves (eg, 'At nursery school we had to play on the floor with bricks —but we didn't have to do sums with them.').

Commentary

1. From the outset the class area is deliberately laid out to be attractive and eye-catching to the children, and to facilitate their circulation and access to equipment and materials. This state of readiness did not arise unheralded. In practical terms, it was created during the previous week when Mrs Robertson spent three full days at school.

2. Mrs Robertson's initial contact with the children is deliberately built on a person-to-person rather than a teacher-to-class basis. This not only makes it easier for her to learn about the children individually but also minimises the chances that they will be overwhelmed by a more formal approach.

3. Although there are only nine children present on the first day, Mrs Robertson is unable to attend to all of them at once. As a result, she tries to provide activities which the children can do with the minimum of direct supervision.

4. The children are deliberately introduced to a set of rules about tidiness; that is, they are taught certain conventions about the use and replacement of equipment. These rules, however, do not necessarily meet with immediate acceptance. They may conflict with patterns of behaviour established elsewhere (eg, at nursery school). Thus, the children may have to unlearn old ideas before they can learn new ones. (All the children come from professional families and have spent at least one year at nursery school.)

5. The children have come to school with all sorts of expectations about what will take place when they get there. To the extent that these expectations are unfulfilled the children may become disoriented. (Interviews with the parents later revealed that disappointment was the most frequent negative reaction shown by the children during the first days of term. For instance, one child (in the words of her mother) was 'bitterly disappointed' that she did not learn to read and write on the first day.)

> At ten past nine Keith asks to draw and is shown the pile of paper on one of the small tables. He sits down and starts crayoning on the top sheet of the pile (thus preventing anyone else from taking paper). Mrs Robertson suggests that he might sit somewhere else. When he has found a new seat she asks him what colour he is using. . . . Michael receives a caution about the level of his 'playground' voice. Mrs Robertson leads Julie and Peter by the hand to show them around the class area. They are taken to the painting area. Douglas is asked to lend Julie his pinafore so that she can paint. Someone finds a piece of jigsaw puzzle on the floor. Emily has found her way into the house and is using the ironing board. Mrs Robertson remarks to the class in general: 'Oh dear, someone doesn't push their chairs in'. She is given some green foliage by Mrs Nuthall who teaches in an adjoining area. Peter is sent to fetch some water. Julie comes back to the class area having finished her painting in four minutes. Just before 9.20am Mrs Robertson asks Michael about his drawing. . . .

Commentary (cont'd)

6. Mrs Robertson continues to encourage the children to find their way around the class and adjacent areas. Her aim is to increase their self-reliance—a necessary condition for the kind of teaching she plans to develop over the following weeks.

7. She also begins to analyse the children's intellectual, social and emotional competence. Such skills are demonstrated, for example, in a child's capacity to remember a list of instructions, to work at a co-operative task, or to cope with the stress of being lost in a strange building.

8. By referring to 'playground voices', Mrs Robertson tries to establish the acceptable noise limits for the class area.

9. Mrs Robertson regards the maintenance of tidiness (ie,

keeping objects in their place and ready for further use) as the personal responsibility of the children. This is a further condition for the development of individualised teaching.

10. In this type of situation a teacher must not only plan for the fact that she cannot attend to all the children at once but also for the fact that the concentration span of each child can be very short.

Keith puts his picture in a schoolbag. Mrs Robertson suggests that he puts it in his drawer. She shows him where the drawer is located. At 9.25am the children are shepherded into the home base. ('What's that?' one of the children asks.) The stragglers receive special reminders ('Are you remembering to put the paint brushes back properly?'). Shortly afterwards a joiner arrives to replace a cupboard lock in the base.

Mrs Robertson changes her plans and takes the children to the unisex toilets. At 9.45am the children return to the home base and Mrs Robertson asks all of them individually about their families. Michael receives a reminder about not interrupting other people. Stephen is sent to look for the milk bottles. The children are lined up and are led to the milk crate. Mrs Robertson asks them to take their milk to an empty table ('We don't want milky plasticine') and then shows the class how to open their bottles. When they have finished she also indicates where they are to put the tops, straws and empty bottles. The children return to their earlier activities. Someone has left out a yellow crayon. Michael finds his way into Mrs Nuthall's area (next to Mrs Robertson's) and works with some toy cars. Other children are shown the outdoor sandpit and are left to work there unsupervised (but overlooked by other teachers).

Commentary (cont'd)

11. Although this episode contains the first occasion when the class are taken as a group, the teacher's attention is still focussed on the attributes of individual children. For the children, however, it becomes a real class (ie, group) situation: while the teacher elicits information about their home circumstances (eg, family size), the children begin to learn how to take their turn in a group discussion.

12. The class teaching later that morning is quite different. The main flow of information is from the teacher to the pupils. In

this sense the children are the receivers of knowledge, whereas previously they were the transmitters.

13. Although, ostensibly, Mrs Robertson merely shows Keith the location of his drawer, her action has much more than transitory significance. First, she is aware that Keith may not be able to read his own name and therefore must learn to recognise his drawer by non-literate means (eg, by its position in the drawer unit). Second, she tries to discourage the children from putting completed work directly into their schoolbags since, at a later stage, she intends to monitor their work before they take it home. (When they start to use notebooks Mrs Robertson will indicate special places in the home base for the children to put work that is to be marked (see Day 10).)

14. Despite being interrupted by the joiner, Mrs Robertson switches without difficulty to another activity. Furthermore, having organised the children into a group for the first time, she deliberately retains this form of organisation rather than letting the children return to their individual activities.

15. At this stage the children have neither learned the 'boundaries' of their class area nor the composition of their class group. Thus, the more adventurous of them take advantage of the attractions to be found in other class areas (and the willingness of other teachers to receive them).

16. The children are deliberately taken to the sandpit since it is not visible from the class area. Mrs Robertson is interested not simply to see whether they can work on their own but also whether they can work at such a distance from the class base.

At 11.35am Mrs Robertson gathers the children together in the home base and tells them the story of the three bears. Some of the children keep interrupting. Eventually Michael is told that 'When I'm telling a story, you sit very quietly and listen. . . .' Before letting the children return to their individual activities, Mrs Robertson reminds them to bring their pinafores the following day. . . . Douglas and Michael become noisy; Mrs Robertson takes them 'for a walk' while the rest of the class continue with their drawing, painting, etc. Meanwhile Miss Dean (another primary one teacher) comes into the area to report that the toilets are awash. When she returns Mrs Robertson takes her entire class back into the toilets and reiterates the correct procedures (eg, 'turn the taps on gently'). At 12.25 the children are asked to find their schoolbags and put on their coats. Peter is sent with Julie to show her how to put off the lights. When the children have gathered in the base Mrs Robertson reminds them about the toilets. Finally, she says a formal 'Good Afternoon' to the children. Their reply is ragged. She asks the children what her name is and then repeats the greeting. Their response is more appropriate. At 12.30 the children pick up their schoolbags and move out into the communal area where their parents are waiting.

Commentary (cont'd)

17. Mrs Robertson's decision to recount a story that the children already know is deliberate. She tells it 'for security, not newness' (see note 2). Nevertheless, this decision also relates to another purpose. As Mrs Robertson expects, some of the children have not yet learned how to listen to a story. Unwittingly they contravene two important rules. First, that listening is a passive activity; and second, that unless their questions are to the point, they should be asked at the end of a story rather than in the middle.

18. Mrs Robertson maintains her policy of talking to the children individually. Thus her reaction to Michael and Douglas's noisy interaction is to take them quietly outside the class area, not to make a public issue of it. Although unsure of the reasons that underly their exceptional behaviour, Mrs Robertson deliberately chooses this course of action. On the basis of her earlier interaction with these boys, she treats their outburst (and her own diagnostic and remedial reaction) as something that is of little relevance to the other children. Had she considered that the boys' behaviour was related to a more general issue (eg, a failure to replace equipment) she might have used the occasion to address the class as a group. As this incident suggests, Mrs Robertson's strategies for maintaining classroom control vary widely from situation to situation. Indeed, the most invisible strategy—that of observation rather than intervention— is probably the most pervasive at this stage in the school year.

19. The pupils' day is built round very short units of time and a generous supply of activities. In catering terms the curriculum is rather like a smorgasbord. The children help themselves from tables laden with attractive dishes produced earlier in the day. This analogy can be extended. The children can sit where they like, 'eat' as much as they like, and follow the courses in any order they like. One effect of this buffet-like arrangement is that the teachers are relatively free to circulate around their own class area and, for similar reasons, to enter each other's teaching areas. (Later in the year, this form of teacher movement becomes less pronounced since, in effect, the buffet is transformed into a more formal dinner party.)

20. By asking Peter to show Julie the location of the light switch, Mrs Robertson begins to capitalise on the fact that the children can teach one another. Again, this is important to her overall style of individualised teaching. She also uses a similar chain-message technique to spread information around the class. For example, she is able to gather the entire group in the home base without ever addressing them publicly.

21. The fact that Mrs Robertson has to take her class for a second formal visit to the toilets is the first evidence that her teaching strategies are not always successful. Repeatedly throughout the year she has to retrace her steps and 'start again'. To the extent that the children's learning is uneven and partial, Mrs Robertson's teaching must be cyclical and reiterative rather than linear and cumulative. On this occasion the children are taken through the same steps as before. On other occasions Mrs Robertson might vary the strategy and use a different route.

22. Mrs Robertson's rehearsal of the formal greeting ('Good afternoon') at the end of the day is not merely for her own benefit. She realises that there will be other occasions in the coming weeks when the children are likely to receive a similar greeting from an unknown (outside) visitor. By stressing this activity, Mrs Robertson hopes not only that the children will be well-prepared for such an eventuality, but also that no one (herself, the visitor, or the children) will find it embarrassing.

FIRST DAYS AT SCHOOL

DAY TWO

(This and later extracts from the fieldnotes have been chosen selectively to illustrate new and changing features of the classroom context.)

By nine o'clock eighteen children are present. Parents are standing in the doorway. Julie stands watching the others. Morag has burst into tears. . . . Three children are drawing, four are working with the plasticine, two are painting, two are building with unifix, one is working with beads, one with a jigsaw and one with a set of wooden dolls. The remaining two children hover around Mrs Robertson. . . . Julie sits alone in the home base reading her birthday book. Morag is looking for Mrs Robertson. Nicola tells the boy sitting next to her that he is 'not allowed' to work with plasticine on the table. . . . Laura (a newcomer) has left a tin of crayons where she was drawing. Julie puts it back with the other tins. A boy from another class looks into the area.

Commentary (cont'd)

23. Mrs Robertson is not surprised that one of the children bursts into tears. Her subsequent action, however, is hampered by her lack of knowledge about Morag. Her response, therefore, can only be one of general reassurance. Later in the year she will be in a much better position to identify the precipitating factors of such behaviour. Through time her responses become much more specific and personal.

24. This episode indicates that the 'old' children have not only learned some of the special rules concerning the use and location of equipment but also have begun to teach them to the newcomers.

At about nine-fifteen Mrs Robertson shows the children who have been working with plasticine what to do when they have finished. In particular, she warns against mixing the colours. Nicola's tea party has turned into 'bathing the baby'. Morag plays with the unifix blocks but eventually leaves them to look for Mrs Robertson who is in the painting area helping Michael to wash his hands. . . . Later, when all the children are gathered in the home base, Mrs Robertson explains the difficulty of removing plasticine from the carpet. Douglas interjects: 'What's that clock for?'. Mrs Robertson takes Morag to the toilet. She fears an 'accident' has happened (it hasn't). The remaining children talk among themselves. When Morag returns Mrs Robertson asks Julie to show Nicola how to put the class light out. All the class are asked about their brothers and sisters. At 9.36am Mrs Robertson begins to teach the children an action game. Michael repeatedly pokes his neighbour and is moved to another place. The group move on to a number game. Morag begins to cry and, at Mrs Robertson's suggestion, moves to sit beside her. Everyone sings 'Happy Birthday' for Julie. Rona shows Stephen the light switch. The 'old' pupils return to their activities while Mrs Robertson takes the new children to the toilet.

Commentary (cont'd)

25. Some children take up more of Mrs Robertson's time than others. Basically this is because they do not fit easily into the type of teaching that she is trying to establish. In some cases, for instance, the children are unable to work without regular supervision; in other cases they are quite capable of independent work but choose to ignore the rules and conventions that are accepted by the other children.

26. The differentiation between 'new' and 'old' children is the first occasion when the class falls into well-defined groups. Nevertheless, this structure is only temporary and will be dissolved by the start of the following week. Generally, Mrs Robertson does not make use of formal groups to organise her teaching but, as above, forms them on a temporary, *ad hoc* basis. Likewise, the location of the 'plasticine table' may move from day to day.

While the new children are at the toilet, Emily and Nicola reconvene the tea party. Michael, Keith, and Douglas join them. A few minutes later (9.53am) Douglas and Michael start a mock knife fight at the tea table. Keith watches and the girls carry on preparing the party. . . . Douglas puts down the knife and starts to pass the toy iron over Michael's hair. . . .The toilet group return and Mrs Robertson reminds the boys in the tea party to behave more appropriately. She then moves into the painting area. The knife fight becomes a sword fight. . . . (10.08am) Douglas moves out of the house and begins to wave his knife in front of Peter who is seated at the plasticine table. Mrs Robertson intervenes, smacks Douglas's bottom once with the palm of her hand ('I'm very cross with you'), and makes him sit on his own. Christina wheels a small pram through the class area while Mrs Robertson reminds the remaining members of the tea party about the noise-level of their 'playground' voices. Mrs Robertson then takes Laura for a walk round the painting area. . . . At milk time (10.20am) Christina asks 'Do we have this every day?'.

Commentary (cont'd)

27. The 'knifefight' and its eventual resolution is a turning point in Mrs Robertson's relationship with Douglas. Her decision to smack him was taken in the light of the knowledge she had accumulated over the preceding two days. On balance she felt that the gravity of the situation justified the intensity of the remedy. Later that day Douglas told his parents about his experience. They came to see Mrs Robertson and, upon hearing her explanation, endorsed the action she had taken. They, too, were concerned about their son's behaviour. While at nursery school Douglas had suffered from asthma. As a consequence, his broken attendance record allowed him to contravene the standards that were normally applied to other children. In addition his nursery teacher had been reluctant to enforce such standards for fear of reactivating the asthma. In the parents' own words (as recorded during an interview) Douglas had become 'uncontrollable' at nursery school. Although he continued to be a regular focus of Mrs Robertson's attention, Douglas's general demeanour became much more subdued after this shared experience.
28. The fact that Mrs Robertson chooses to take Laura into the painting area illustrates a dramatic shift in her attention. Unlike Douglas, Laura does not place any overt demands on the teacher (see Note 25). Nevertheless, Mrs Robertson is quite aware that Laura has not previously shown any apparent desire to paint. Thus, although certain children apparently receive more attention than others, this does not necessarily mean that the remaining children are beyond Mrs Robertson's field of vision.
29. Christina's question 'Do we have this every day?' indicates that while some children (especially those with older brothers and sisters) may be fully conversant with the nature and conventions of schooling (see Note 5), there are others who find it a significant

source of wonder and amazement. At times Mrs Robertson builds upon this atmosphere of fantasy and mystery. She feels that is a useful way to excite the children's curiosity and thereby retain their attention. For instance, each number (1, 2, 3, etc) is introduced to the children with a story which features a character or object of that shape. In the case of the figure 2, the story is about a swan (see also Note 40).

DAY THREE

At 8.30am Stephen works with the plasticine while Mrs Robertson moves the tables to give better access to the bricks. David arrives with a group of other children. Nicola bursts into tears. Christina tries to befriend her but is rejected. Douglas starts to paint. David works with a puzzle on the high table. Mrs Robertson asks him to sit at a low table or to take it on the floor. (8.45am) Mrs Robertson and Christina discuss the previous day's events over the telephone. Nicola (now recovered) takes over at Mrs Robertson's end. Several new parents arrive at once. Keith shows his father where his schoolbag is kept. Simon wanders about carrying a tub of plasticine. Julie arrives clutching her birthday cards. Michael instructs a new boy on the use of crayons ('Take a whole box; take a whole box'). (8.57am) The entire class are present for the first time (10 girls, 13 boys). David returns the jigsaw puzzle with the pieces dismantled.

Commentary (cont'd)

30. Mrs Robertson moves the furniture about since, specifically, none of the children have yet used the bricks that are stored in a corner. This strategy also eases the demands that the increased class size places upon the existing equipment. In general, Mrs Robertson deliberately arranges (and rearranges) her class area to make the best educational use of the available resources. In this sense her teaching is quite consciously interventionist. Some areas are made more accessible than others, some equipment is brought out from the cupboard, some items are hidden away (see Day Ten).

31. By this stage in the year some children have already internalised the ruling conventions of the class area. As far as

Mrs Robertson is concerned this is a mixed blessing. The children begin to feel at home but at the same time also begin to show signs of restlessness and disenchantment. For this reason, if no other, Mrs Robertson tries to schedule her work at this stage so that something new appears in each day's work programme (see Note 29).

32. Just as Mrs Robertson learns about the children, they also learn about each other. Friendships and social groupings begin to be formed.

(9.02am) Mrs Robertson walks round the tables and asks the children to tidy up and go into the home base. The experienced class members are asked to help the new ones. Emily tells her neighbour: 'You have to push your chair in'. Ewan points towards the home base and asks 'Is that it?'. A boy and a girl from another class come into the area and ask Mrs Robertson if they can paint. . . . (9.08am) In the home base, Mrs Robertson reiterates her jigsaw policy (viz. they should be replaced on the high table but not before they have been reassembled). She then says a formal 'Good Morning' to the class and, for the first time, marks up the register. When Julie (the second person on the register) is asked 'Are you here?' she pauses and then replies 'Yes' in a tone of voice that suggests she finds the question totally pointless. (As if to say: 'Yes, of course I'm here today'.) After registration, Colin is asked whether his brother is older or younger than himself. He is unable to reply. 'Is he bigger or smaller than you?'. Colin gives an answer. . . . Mrs Robertson reads the "Mr Happy" story to the class. There are very few random interruptions although some children mistake pauses in the story for invitations to ask questions. . . . (9.26am) The experienced children are told about choosing their activities: 'You don't need to ask. If you want to paint and there's an easel free . . .'. Morag starts to cry and is taken on to Mrs Robertson's lap.

Commentary (cont'd)

33. The arrival of two children from another class to ask if they can paint reinforces the idea that the children have not yet developed a strong sense of classness.

34. Julie's amazement at being asked 'Are you here?' when Mrs Robertson marks the register is a unique event never to be

repeated in the context of that class. By the time the registration has been completed she has learned—like all the others—how to give the appropriate response ('Yes, Mrs Robertson'). At all levels, teaching is characterised by the repeated use of 'pseudo questions' (ie, questions which are not designed to be treated literally). As this illustration indicates, children are not always aware of the real meaning of these questions. At the same time, however, it also reveals that, if shown, they can rapidly learn their real purpose.

35. The discussion between Mrs Robertson and Colin about his family is a good illustration of the fact that discourse between teachers and pupils is multi-layered. For the teacher's part she not only learns about Colin's home setting but also about his competence with mathematical relationships, his knowledge about family structure (eg, brother, sister), and his ability to keep to the point of a discussion.

36. This is the first time that Mrs Robertson reads a new story to the children. To control them without constantly interrupting the story Mrs Robertson varies the inflection of her voice. Nevertheless, some children still misunderstand the messages that she conveys by this means. Her dramatic pauses are sometimes taken to be opportunities to ask questions.

DAY FIVE

9.28am (in the home base). Mrs Robertson produces 'Hamish' (a matchstick man made from pipe cleaners). She then gives each child a book made of sheets of drawing paper stapled together. Different shapes have already been traced out at the top of the pages in the book. The children leave the home base, put their books on the small tables and then sit on the floor facing the blackboard. David has to be reminded to put his book on a table. Mrs Robertson leads the children in making shapes in the air. The children then return to their seats. Christina points to her name on the book and asks Mary 'What does that say?'. Douglas and Nicola begin to trace out the shapes using crayons. Mrs Robertson interrupts them. They are asked to put their crayons back in the tins and, with the rest of the class, put their hands on their laps. The children are requested to point to their names at the top of the page. Mrs Robertson scans the class. David has his book upside down. Three children are moved to different seats (so that all the left-handed children sit together). David has already started. The children are asked to choose a pencil and trace out the shapes, starting from 'Hamish's red dot' (a matchstick man marker on the left-hand side of the page). When the children have finished Mrs Robertson demonstrates the next exercise on the blackboard. . . . (9.48am) The children are then asked to sit on the floor around the drawer units. . . . Each child has the same number on their tray as on their writing book. One by one they put their books away under Mrs Robertson's supervision.

Commentary (cont'd)

37. The distribution of writing materials represents the first time that the children are seated as a class group for a book orientated activity. For approximately the next ten days Mrs Robertson uses this all-class approach for the introduction of new topics. It is the 'dinner party' curriculum referred to earlier (see Note 19). A fixed, no-choice menu is followed by all the pupils in a definite sequence. The teacher sits at the head of the 'table' and the courses are brought out at the same time for each child.
38. Although Mrs Robertson has spent a great deal of time in preparing this writing activity, not everything goes to plan. Nevertheless, this outcome is not entirely unexpected. Each time she has previously introduced this topic it has produced new and unforeseen difficulties. Mrs Robertson is quite prepared, therefore, for the widely different degrees of competence shown by the children. However, to bring the activity to a relatively tidy conclusion, Mrs Robertson deliberately chooses a follow-up activity which retains the whole-class form of organisation (see Note 14) but which, by contrast, is relatively simple and easily completed.
39. During this episode (which lasts less than twenty-five minutes) Mrs Robertson moves the whole class through four different positions (home base, in front of blackboard, seated at tables, in front of drawer units). She makes the maximum use of available space but, most of the time, keeps the children very close to her. Again this has implications for the monitoring and control of individual children. By her close proximity to the children, Mrs Robertson can see and hear much more than in a

dispersed situation. For the same reasons, her own behaviour is much more visible to the rest of the class. Furthermore, in this position she can use techniques (eg, touching children) which are inevitably (or conventionally) ruled out in a dispersed teaching situation.

40. Mrs Robertson's use of 'Hamish' to show the children where to start writing illustrates the strategy of building upon their sense of fantasy.

> At 10 o'clock six children are asked to sit on the floor by the blackboard. The others are asked if they want to paint. Douglas asks Mrs Robertson what he might do; she gives him a shapes board. Mrs Robertson then moves the group of six to the window where they are given boxes of tokens and toys to sort out into different groups. They do this while she attends to the rest of the class. (10.12am) Mrs Robertson asks the sorting group, one by one, to count out the groups they have prepared (eg, three flowers, four peas, . . . etc). She keeps a record of their achievements. (10.25am) Mrs Robertson announces that this will be the last time that the class take their milk all together. She explains that in future the children can take their milk whenever they wish. Michael asks 'What happens if we don't know when to go?'. When Michael has finished his milk Mrs Robertson talks to him about the grouping exercise. When he asks 'What is maths?' all of a sudden, someone else replies 'work'. After milk the class are assembled in front of the blackboard and then introduced to 'Dick'—a cardboard figure stuck to a magnetic board. Mrs Robertson writes 'Dick' on the blackboard and asks the children what it says. She then tries 'dock' and 'dish'. . . . While the class are putting on their coats to go out to playtime, Michael bursts into tears: 'I want mummy'. . . . (11.50am) Mrs Robertson requests the class to 'Stop and listen' (twice). She then asks the children to try to work more quietly. . . . David, James and John re-enact a minor war with the wood blocks. (12.00) Mrs Robertson goes round the class area asking the children to move into the home base. When the children are ready she takes them round the class area pointing out where the class rules have been ignored—library, telephone table, games table, and class chairs.

Commentary (cont'd)

41. The teaching groups that are formed to sort out the counters

have no other purpose and are disbanded immediately afterwards. Nevertheless, they represent the emergence of specialist group activities organised around tasks deliberately set by the teacher. The importance of this activity is underlined by the fact that Mrs Robertson keeps a written record of the results.

42. Day five is the last occasion when the children take their milk all together as a class. As far as milk consumption is concerned, the 'dinner party' is over. On subsequent days the children follow a self-service system and take their milk whenever they wish. The patterns of class organisation that Mrs Robertson uses at milk time tend to run ahead of those used for other activities. Thus, the whole class consumption of milk is abandoned at a time when such patterns are just being introduced for other activities.

43. Although the children have already begun to learn the basic skills of writing, this is the first occasion when they are required to recognise word shapes (a prerequisite for reading). Furthermore, this is the first time that Mrs Robertson has written on the blackboard; a cogent reminder that it is a literate medium.

44. When Michael burst into tears at playtime he has misunderstood the nature of the occasion. The fact that the other children were putting on their coats reminds him of home time. He has not fully learned the routine of the school day.

45. Of the nine days' observation this proved to be the most tearful. Six children cried at some time during the day (Monday). Mrs Robertson had predicted this state of affairs and attributed it to the fact that the weekend had given the children the opportunity to forget about school. In this sense some of the children had to re-start school—but in the context of a much larger group, and a much more crowded class area. In a more general sense Mrs Robertson felt that these events marked the start-of-term 'crisis'—a turning point in the first few days of every school year.

46. Mrs Robertson's double call for the children to 'Stop and listen' and her subsequent reiteration of the classroom rules is one indication of the fragile stability of classroom life. Although at any given time the overall atmosphere may appear to be stable it is, in fact, more accurate to characterise it as a state of continual oscillation: at times the children set the pace, at other

times it is the teacher who takes the initiative. On this occasion Mrs Robertson feels that the children are moving too far ahead of her. To restore the balance, she decides to remind them of the core rules that govern the use of furniture and equipment.

DAY SIX

(9.26am) After telling Mrs Robertson their news the children listen to a story in silence. Shortly after 9.30am the children are asked to fetch their writing books from their trays and find a seat. While Mrs Robertson walks round the class checking that the children have the right book, Keith, Michael, and Rona discuss the significance of the numbers at the top of their books. Mrs Robertson asks the class to turn to page two. Several children turn the book over completely. When the class is quiet Mrs Robertson asks 'What is the first thing to do?' ('Look for Hamish'). On this occasion the left-handed group no longer sit together. When the children are left to finish the tracing exercise Julie starts one of the lines with the crayon in her right hand and finishes it left-handed. As a second number group is being convened by Mrs Robertson, Ewan asks if he can go to the sand. He is told that he can choose for himself. . . . When the number group breaks up Emily tells them that 'We've had our milk'. . . .

Commentary (cont'd)
47. Although this is the second occasion that the children have used their writing books, they still find difficulty in making sense of them. (Indeed, when the children eventually come to the end of the eight-page books, Mrs Robertson decided to prepare another version to repeat the earlier practice.)
48. Now that Mrs Robertson has observed the left-handed children in a writing situation she no longer requires them to sit together (see Note 26).
49. Gradually the children learn the appropriate strategies to follow in the class area. At the same time they also learn the specialised words that are used to describe the strategies (eg, 'choosing').

DAY NINE

Over and above the regular choosing activities the children complete the last page of the writing book. Emily complains that she hasn't got a page eight (she has) and David writes on the wrong page. . . . A final sorting group is convened. . . . At 10.20am Mrs Robertson rehearses the number work that she has introduced on previous days. 'How do we make one?'. The children chant 'down' and make an imaginary stroke in the air. She then brings out a set of cards featuring the number 'two'. When the children have answered her questions (eg, 'How many boots are there? How many eyes has the cat?'), she makes them practice the shape in the air. Before letting the children find a seat to work at, Mrs Robertson distributes the number books by holding them up and waiting to see if the children can recognise their own names. The number books are very similar to the writing books. They are home-made by the teacher and comprise spirit-duplicated sheets stapled together by Mrs Lee, the auxiliary. The children trace out the number shapes page by page and also use their crayons to colour the diagrams that go with them. This activity continues after playtime. . . . After a further period of choosing, the children gather again in the home base. Mrs Robertson continues to tell them about the seasonal events of autumn (eg, fruits and seeds). While the children are still in the home base, she introduces them to 'Fluff' (the cat owned by Dick and Dora). She then sits by the magnetic board and 'plays a game' with the children by matching (and mismatching) the words against the pictures (Dick, Dora, Nip (the dog), and Fluff). The children correct her when she makes a mistake. Andrew asks if they will be 'getting Dick and Dora books'. When Mrs Robertson sends the class to fetch the colouring boks from their trays there is a period of confusion since not all the children find the correct book (ie, the one with their name on it). The children are asked to colour in one picture of Fluff and one of Nip. There is some difficulty because there are not enough black and brown crayons to go round all the children. (12.15) Some of the children have finished so Mrs Robertson asks them to take their schoolbags to their seats. Colin complains that James is sitting in his seat. Mrs Robertson explains that he doesn't have his own seat. He finds another but wanders out of it. Morag takes it. Colin returns to say to Morag: 'I was there first'. Mrs Robertson helps Morag to find a new seat. . . .

Commentary (cont'd)
50. The fact that the number activity spreads over playtime is

the first occasion that Mrs Robertson has allowed this to occur. Previously all class activities have been drawn to a conclusion before the children go out to play.

51. Three different kinds of classroom procedures co-exist at this time: individual choosing, specialist groups, and whole class teaching. As shown earlier (see Note 42) these procedures are not insulated from each other. At different times they will be applied to the same part of the curriculum. For instance, children may learn to write as a class but later receive group or even individual tuition. Later still, writing may become a 'choosing' activity.

52. The confusion that emerges when the children fetch the colouring books from their trays arises from the fact that it is the first time that they have been asked, as a class, to fetch anything from their trays. Previously, Mrs Robertson has given the books out individually to each child.

53. The episode when there were not enough black and brown crayons for all the children to use them is a specific but rare instance where the teaching strategy used by Mrs Robertson runs up against a (relative) shortage of resources. The most visible outcome in this type of situation is that the children are forced to wait their turn. In most instances Mrs Robertson pre-empts this type of queuing by forethought and suitable planning. Furthermore, if it does arise she is usually able to prevent its reaching disruptive proportions by the redirection of children or resources.

54. The seating policy followed by Mrs Robertson is that the children can sit wherever they wish. (The only time this convention is breached is when she asks individual children to sit on their own—usually because they have been interfering with someone else's work.) Thus, each child may use several work places during the day. In these terms it is an exceptional occurrence for Colin to complain that his seat has been taken. What in fact happened was that his temporary seat reservation (marked by his schoolbag on the table) was, inadvertently, double-booked by another child. Colin's general behaviour suggests that perhaps his nursery school was organised around the idea that every child has their own chair. Thus, before he can learn the new regime he must unlearn the old one (see Note 4).

DAY TEN

(9.37am) While Mrs Robertson gives out a set of new (home-made) books, Julie puts a tin of crayons on each table. . . . The front page of the books has drawings of Dick, Dora, Nip and Fluff with their names on the right-hand side of the page but not directly opposite the drawing. The children are shown how to draw a line between the picture and the correct word. . . . Mrs Robertson calls out the names of the children who are to join her when they have finished their matching books: the remainder are left to choose. . . . Some children can't find the right colour crayon to colour Dick etc. Mrs Robertson stops the class, asks them to put their crayons back in the tins and then impresses upon them that they are to work quietly. . . . (10am) Ewan finishes, puts his book in the base to be marked and then goes to find the telephone (which Mrs Robertson has deliberately removed from the class area). Laura asks 'What do we choose?'. At Colin's suggestion they both go to the milk table and drink their milk. Some children have forgotten whether they are to choose or to wait for Mrs Robertson. Laura is wandering about; Mrs Robertson takes her to the painting area but finds she doesn't want to paint. Mrs Robertson looks for Mrs Lee (the auxiliary) as some of the paints are missing. Meanwhile the special group have assembled near the blackboard. (10.08am) After an initial briefing, the group return to their tables. Mrs Robertson holds up shapes (a circle, a square, etc) which they copy on to individual sheets of paper divided into four quarters.

Commentary (cont'd)

55. The word and picture matching exercise did not emerge unheralded; it had already been foreshadowed by the home base activity of the previous day.

56. In several aspects, this thirty-minute episode of classroom life did not develop as Mrs Robertson had hoped. For instance, many children forgot the detailed instructions about what they were to do after the matching exercise. As a result the children sought guidance from each other or from Mrs Robertson. Inevitably, the noise level increased. (Much later in the year Mrs Robertson avoided this type of problem by writing the work instructions on the blackboard.) Similarly, Laura's (unanswer-

able) question: 'What do we chose?' indicates that not only was she unsure of the available options but also (as shown by her behaviour in the painting area) that she was unattracted by some of those that were most visible.

57. The shortage of paints draws attention to the role of the school auxiliaries. (Three are shared among fifteen classes.) Like many of the support services in education their importance only becomes apparent when the system fails to function. In practice Mrs Lee carries out many of the organisational and planning tasks that would otherwise fall to Mrs Robertson. In effect, she underwrites many of the processes that are intrinsic to the type of teaching methods used by Mrs Robertson. (During the rest of the term the children gradually learn to distinguish Mrs Robertson from Mrs Lee and, at the same time, gradually learn to go directly to Mrs Lee when they need the assistance which she can provide. Through Mrs Lee's help Mrs Robertson can focus more continuously on working with individual children.)

DAY TWELVE

(9.36am) The class sits around the board which has 'Here is' written on it. Mrs Robertson completes the sentence by adding Dick etc. The children read out the full sentence. They are then introduced to a new word: 'Mummy'. Mrs Robertson draws a series of balloons on the board. She asks individual children to read the words written in the balloons. If they can, they are asked to 'blow the balloons away' (ie, they are rubbed out). . . . (9.45am) Mrs Robertson introduces the children to the word 'assignment'. She takes a pile of 'everyday' books and shows the children that 'You've all got different things to do' (the tasks are already written into the books by Mrs Robertson). Rona asks to go to the toilet. The class are told that when they've finished their everyday books they are to put them on the pile and then 'choose'. (9.58am) While the rest of the class work at the tables, Keith, Julie and Michael have a session with Mrs Robertson and their 'matchbox' words (individual words written on small pieces of card that the children keep in a matchbox and take home to their parents).

FIRST DAYS AT SCHOOL

Commentary (cont'd)

58. The introduction of the assignment (a daily work schedule) marks another shift in the kind of teaching used by Mrs Robertson. The children are being introduced to the individualised (or better still, personalised) curriculum which will gradually displace, but not entirely replace, the smorgasbord and dinner party curricula introduced earlier. In effect, the children begin to follow specially prepared individual diets which complement the more staple fare offered by the accessible smorgasbord and the formal dinner party.

59. The reading words not only mark the introduction of homework but also provide the children with a visible school-based criterion for differentiating among themselves (eg, 'How many words have you got?'). Although Mrs Robertson tries to avoid this outcome by giving each child four pieces of card (some with repeat words), the children soon discover their relative levels of progress. Later, this differentiation becomes even more visible when the children move on to their first reading book. Thus, the children not only begin to read but also begin to cope with a set of more pervasive school-based ideas about success and failure, cooperation and competition, work and play.

> (The schoolday continues.) Morag comes out to Mrs Robertson as she cannot find the place in her everyday book. Emily is reminded that if she does not know what to do, she is not to call out but, instead, sit and wait beside Mrs Robertson. Michael has difficulty in distinguishing 'Dick' from 'Dora' (his new word). Shortly afterwards he is sent to call up Simon but the message does not arrive. Children start going out to Mrs Robertson. The register boy arrives. (10.30am) Colin is chastised for interrupting Mrs Robertson. Eight children are still working in their everyday books. David has started writing on a random page in his book but is redirected to the correct page. Morag takes her book for Mrs Robertson's inspection but is told 'You don't really need to bring it to me . . . put it on the pile'. Christina and William are hovering around outside Mrs Lee's room—waiting for paint. Mrs Robertson gets up and goes to find out their difficulty. She takes Lucy and Stephen to the sandpit. (Stephen has been on his own but has found the door locked.) Back at the blackboard Mrs Robertson listens to Andrew and Rona

read. Simon asks to go to the toilet. Stephen complains that Keith has interrupted his work with the bricks. . . . At 10.20am the class are engaged on the following activities: building with woodblocks (6), milk (1), painting (3), jigsaw puzzles (2), unifix blocks (4), drawing (3), reading (1), observing (2). . . .

Commentary (cont'd)
60. This final extract from the fieldnotes is deliberately left unabridged. It is included to underline the fact that although Mrs Robertson's teaching is individualised, she also has responsibility for up to twenty-two other children at the same time. Thus, before she can develop person-to-person teaching she must also design activities for the rest of the class. In this sense her overall unit of organisation still remains the entire teaching group, not the individual child.

DISCUSSION

In certain respects the practice of teaching is like the art of cooking. It involves the transformation of a set of ingredients (the syllabus) into a finished product (the daily work programme) by means of a set of procedures (the teaching methods). Yet teaching is rather more than the application of recipe knowledge. Competence is not unequivocably guaranteed by the terms of the cookbook. Other background skills are also relevant.

The final section of this essay focuses on this aspect of teaching. That is, it considers some of the 'intangibles' (here described as preparation, experience, continuity, vision, and responsiveness) which might help to differentiate the work of a competent teacher from that of a trainee.

Preparation
One central if not paradoxical feature of Mrs Robertson's work is that much of it takes place when the children are not at school. In short, the form and content of her classroom activities are made possible only by a considerable amount of off-stage preparation.

This preparation takes different forms. Its most visible aspect relates to the day-by-day maintenance of the work programme. Preparation of this type encompasses taken-for-granted activities such as the marking of books or the repair and replacement of damaged or disposable equipment. Less frequently—but perhaps more significantly—Mrs Robertson's preparation is also directed towards a qualitative change in the day-to-day routine. This second kind of preparation is reflected in the rearrangement of furniture, the introduction of novel materials (eg, TV broadcasts), or in the rehearsal of new techniques (eg, the dinner party curriculum). A third type of preparation probably occurs least often but requires the greatest amount of intellectual investment. It relates to the development of classroom activities which are as new to the teacher as they are to the children. In such an instance the teacher has chosen to branch out into relatively ill-defined and risk-laden territory.

The difference between these types of preparation is not so much in the activities themselves as in the degree of experience brought to them by the teacher. Student teachers, for example, may find an element of risk in all their preparatory activities whereas unadventurous teachers might never stray beyond the well-defined boundaries of their own experience.

Experience

An important adjunct to preparation is the existence of prior experience. Mrs Robertson's teaching, for example, is not merely the outcome of her more immediate preparation but also the result of her initial training, her five years' experience in the same school, and her regular attendance on in-service courses.

In general, however, experience is not something that automatically accumulates with the passage of time. Changed circumstances can always neutralise the rehearsal value of earlier experience. Whenever Mrs Robertson decides to try out new strategies or whenever her teaching is interrupted by outside events, she puts the value of her previous experience to the test. Sometimes she is able to keep the resultant activities within the realms of her existing knowledge; at other times she is forced to traverse across unknown terrain. Thus, to the extent that it changes or is induced to change, Mrs Robertson's teaching **always contains an element of inexperience.**

Nevertheless, the advantages of appropriate experience cannot be ignored. In Mrs Robertson's case, there are three distinct benefits which accrue to her from previous years. First, she has already fully rehearsed many of the actions that she undertakes day by day. As a result her teaching operates within a set of carefully understood limitations and therefore takes careful account of the availability and accessibility of resources. Second, Mrs Robertson's varied experience gives her a wide repertoire of options to draw upon. Thus, if her plans go awry she can readily switch to another well-tried activity. Finally, Mrs Robertson's experience also gives her a better idea of the consequences of her actions; she can weigh each alternative in the light of its likely outcomes.

Continuity

This potential ability to foresee the results of her decisions introduces a strong thread of continuity into Mrs Robertson's teaching. She realises that each decision may create new situations which require further decisions. To this extent, teaching is not about making 'one-off' decisions but making chains of decisions.

The fact that one decision merely leads to another also relates to a teacher's sense of achievement. Even if Mrs Robertson reaches her immediate goal she knows that there are still other peaks to climb. Likewise she realises that each success may be only shortlived. In this sense a teacher's work is never done. Necessarily, achievement becomes a much more fluid entity. It is not so much the attainment of isolated curriculum objectives as the overall maintenance of continuity, coherence, and progress.

Vision

Although a set of specific objectives are central to Mrs Robertson's work programme, they are not the sole basis of her educational strategy. The major steering influence is provided by a much larger set of more diffuse and long-term goals. These more distant goals—relating to the general social, intellectual and emotional development of her pupils—are more difficult to specify but are of equal importance to the entire process. Without them, the day-to-day objectives would be meaningless (eg, word recognition is not an end in itself but a means to a more elaborate end). In these terms competent teachers are marked out not so much by their detailed knowledge of separate curricular milestones but by their understanding of the relationship between these and the more long-term goals. The possession of this latter skill—demonstrated by an over-riding sense of direction and purpose—makes it much easier for a teacher to overcome irritating holdups, negotiate awkward diversions and anticipate oncoming obstacles. Competence is a matter of perspective: the ability to visualise the entire forest, not just the individual trees.

Responsiveness

Armed with this understanding a competent teacher can more readily respond to interruptions and diversions. Unplanned occurrences need not be treated as failures; they can become potential growth points. The wisdom of experience and preparation (as demonstrated, quintessentially, by a teacher's sense of timing) can transform unexpected outcomes into new sources of learning and innovation.

Here, as elsewhere it is a capacity to confront the unknown that, for teachers and pupils alike, differentiates competence from incompetence, education from instruction.

Further Reading

For comparable accounts which also share an interest in the micro-processes of teaching and learning see P W Jackson, *Life in Classrooms* (New York: Holt Rinehart & Winston, 1968); L M Smith & W Geoffrey, *The Complexities of an Urban Classroom* (New York: Holt Rinehart & Winston, 1968); and R Walker & C Adelman, *A Guide to Classroom Observation* (London: Methuen, 1975).

5

THE CASE OF THE MISSING CHAIRS

> *"The structures of the open classroom . . . are designed to meet needs that the structures of the conventional classroom cannot fulfil. But prescriptions for structure alone do not tell us how the work of the classroom . . . can be performed."*
>
> (Ian Westbury, *Educationalist*.)[1]

This essay is about the relationship between teaching methods and material resources. It focuses on a recent suggestion that a modern primary school can be organised around less than one chair per pupil. Overall, the essay does not find fault with the motives that prompted such a suggestion. It does, however, find inconsistencies in its logic.

There is a school of thought in primary education which argues that there is no need to provide every child with a seat or a work surface. Support for this idea comes from various sources. New schools find the concept financially acceptable since it releases money from an otherwise fixed grant for the purchase of specialist furnishings such as display screens, storage units and mobile trolleys. Architects endorse the idea since the resultant increase in free space enables them to create more flexible designs. And finally, educationalists lend their weight to the scheme since it visibly undermines a long tradition of class (ie, whole group) teaching.

---

[1] I Westbury, 'Conventional classrooms, open classrooms, and the technology of teaching', *Journal of Curriculum Studies,* Vol 5 (1973), pp 118-9.

The force of these economic, architectural and educational arguments has been considerable. According to one recent English review: 'new purpose-built open-plan schools rarely contain seating accommodation for more than about seventy per cent of the children at any one time'.[2] Not all practitioners, however, have found this innovation educationally acceptable. As a result, chairs and tables—like many other elements in the modern primary school—have become the object of prolonged and often emotive debate. Superficially, the arguments and counter-arguments are about the allocation of financial resources and the utilisation of available space. At a deeper level, however, they also interact with more fundamental concerns about the theory and practice of primary education. In short, discussions about tables and chairs are also debates about methods and curricula.

The first part of this essay explores the origins and assumptions of these debates. The second part relates their logic to the experience of the case-study school. Throughout, two questions are considered:
1. What are the shifts in educational thinking that have given rise to these discussions?
2. How do these shifts relate to a reduced provision of chairs?

The standard answer to these questions is that a lowered requirement of chairs follows automatically from a weaker emphasis upon class and jotter-based teaching. The experience of the case-study school (and the argument of this essay) is that the case for this innovation is weak and inconclusive.

ORIGINS AND ASSUMPTIONS

Debates about educational furnishings and fittings have a long history. Typically, they reflect disagreements about the most appropriate furniture for a given teaching method or curriculum. In 1725 the master of St Andrew's Grammar School complained to the local council that, for lack of suitable writing surfaces, his pupils were obliged to 'wreatt upon the floor lying on their bellies'. At that time writing was considered a major (and somewhat suspect) curriculum innovation. Even by the early nine-

---

[2] K Rintoul and K Thorne, *Open-plan Organisation in the Primary School* (London: Ward Locke Educational, 1975), p 11.

teenth century seats were still regarded as peripheral to curricula which emphasised reading rather than writing. One of the selling points of the monitorial system, for instance, was that only 50 per cent of the pupils needed seats at any one time. (Each half of the class took it in turns to stand in groups and be 'drilled' by the pupil monitors while the other half sat on benches and practised their 'ciphering'.)

Further controversies arose in the late nineteenth century with the development of textbook curricula. During that period not all schools provided suitable 'locker' desks for the storage of books and writing implements.[3]

In turn, however, the heavy locker desks of the elementary school also fell out of favour. By the 1930s it was held that they were too cumbersome or ill-shapen for the 'activity' methods officially advocated as suitable for young children. Nevertheless, locker desks survived until well after the Second World War—though for economic rather than educational reasons.

In the 1950s, a rise in the birth rate triggered a new demand. School furnishings—like new school buildings— began to be designed with an explicit concern for compactness, flexibility, and appropriateness of size. Standardised modules, interchangeable components and child-proof materials became key-note features. Showpiece schools of the 1960s like Eveline Lowe (London) and Kirkhill (West Lothian) deliberately incorporated these new developments as part of their total design. Nevertheless, according to the official reports, the specification of chairs for these schools remained at the figure of 100 per cent.

Chairs—A Vanishing Resource?

At some point in the late 1960s (or so it appears) the idea began to circulate that a primary school could be efficiently furnished with less than 100 per cent seating. The source of this notion is as yet obscure. The fact that there are no references to it in either the Plowden Report (1967) or the Scottish Education Department 'Primary Memorandum' (1965) suggests that it may have been a grass-roots or even an imported idea.

[3] The examples are taken from J Grant, *History of the Burgh and Parish Schools of Scotland*, Vol 1 (London: Collins, 1876), pp 515 and 521.

The rationale for limiting the number of chairs in a school derives from three assumptions:

1. That the basic unit of teaching should be the individual child rather than the whole group.
2. That it is possible to organise work programmes whereby children can be employed on different activities.
3. That not all learning activities require a chair.

There are two problems with this rationale. First, none of these assumptions specifically requires that the provision of seats should be fixed at less than 100 per cent. In fact, it would be possible for a teacher to accept all three ideas and still legitimately demand a full complement of chairs. This would follow, for example, if she added a fourth assumption: that children should be free to choose their own sequence through the various activities of their work programme. Indeed, if a teacher considered this last assumption to be the most important, then it would definitely rule out a reduced provision of chairs. The freedom of individual choice would, by necessity, include the freedom for an entire class to choose a seated activity. Thus, to restrict the number of chairs in a school is automatically to limit the number of curriculum options open to teachers and pupils. Certainly, an increase of chairs may also produce a shortage of usable floor space; but this is not an equivalent problem. Space can be created more easily than extra seating.

The second problem surrounds the levels of seating that are usually considered to be optimum. Although a figure of 60 or 70 per cent is usually quoted, the derivation of these percentages is as obscure as the origins of the initial idea. It is sometimes stated that a 66 per cent (ie, two-thirds) seating level fits easily where classes are sub-divided into three groups. In such cases the expectation is that two-thirds of the class group will need chairs whereas one third will be working at non-seated activities or out of the class area.[4] On balance such an explanation is inadequate. It does not justify the choice of three

---

[4] This rationale is documented in G M Werner, *Policies of School Building Design*, MSocSc thesis (Edinburgh University, 1974).

groups or indicate how a policy of grouping squares with the assumption that the individual child should be the basic teaching unit. (By the same token it would be just as reasonable to divide the class into four groups and have a seating level of 75—or even 50—per cent.)

Given the educational weakness of the foregoing argument, an alternative possibility for the quoted figures is that they derive from the application of a standard architectural formula. By this means a school's optimum seating requirements are calculated in the same manner as the size of its playground and staffroom. Nevertheless, these requirements cannot be predicted unambiguously. They also depend on the kind of educational policy followed by the school. An optimum figure in one situation may be totally inappropriate in another.

Accidental Dissemination?

The rather hybrid nature of these ideas about seating levels suggests that they may have come into being for no other purpose than to focus attention on out-of-date classroom procedures. That is, they were formulated primarily to draw attention to the shortcomings of educational practice, not as a model for changing it. There is a historical parallel for this explanation. The call for a reduced provision of seats in a school is analogous to the rallying cry of an earlier generation that locker desks should be unscrewed from the classroom floor.[5]

If this last explanation is, in fact, correct, then the initial adoption of reduced seating levels may have been an accident— the reluctant or ill-informed act of a financially hardpressed adviser or administrator.

Whatever their origins, the rapid and widespread dissemination of these ideas is almost certainly attributable to the concerted pressure of administrators, college lecturers and architects— three of the most powerful groups in primary education. Although acting for different reasons—expediency, conviction, or

---

[1] For evidence of this movement see: R J D Selleck, *English Primary Education and the Progressives, 1914-39* (London: Routlege and Kegan Paul, 1972), p 54.

functional utility—their combined advocacy has been considerable.

THE CASE-STUDY SCHOOL

In the early 1970s teachers from the case-study school attended a local college of education for courses leading to the Frobel (early education) certificate. During those years, they first encountered the idea that a primary school class might be organised around less than 100 per cent seating. At that time, however, the issue was of academic rather than practical concern, a matter for staffroom discussion rather than school-wide decision.

In 1973 the situation changed. The plans for the new lower primary building had reached the stage where a seating level had to be decided. Consensus among the staff was difficult to achieve since individual members reacted differently to the idea that seating levels might be reduced below one chair per child. Basically, three viewpoints were expressed. One (small) group of teachers were prepared to put their beliefs to the test and try out the idea. A second group (probably the majority) accepted the general notion of a reduced provision but felt that their own situation constituted a special case. (For example, one teacher argued that she preferred to teach writing by means of class lessons.) A third group of teachers were less easily converted. They felt reluctant to abandon either the principle or the practice of providing a full complement of seats for their children. A characteristic feature of this last group was that they felt it was educationally important for each child to have his 'own' chair.

To resolve this issue the headmaster of the school was asked to act as an arbitrator. By his decision the seating level was duly fixed at 60 per cent. In principle this action closed the debate. In practice, however, the teachers were left with a possible alternative: if the designated seating level proved inadequate, it could still be topped up with infant-sized furniture left over from the old building. The flexibility of this arrangement became apparent when some of the ordered furniture failed to arrive in time for the opening of the new building. The old tables and chairs were immediately pressed into service and, in a complete reversal of the original intention, were 'topped up' by the new furniture as it arrived. The eventual surplus of chairs meant that each teacher could operate their own seating policy. Some chose the figure of 60 per cent while others retained at least one chair for each child.

This arrangement did not last for very long. Within a term all the teachers had built up their seating levels to at least 100 per cent. The topping up, however, did not herald a return to class teaching. Quite the reverse: as shown below it marked a recognition that an adequate supply of chairs was necessary to the individualised and balanced curriculum that the case-study teachers were trying to implement. Thus, despite a certain sense of public failure among the teachers who tried to work with a reduced provision, the intervening experience had taught them a great deal about the relationship between teaching methods and seating requirements.

At Classroom Level

The teachers who found themselves unable to operate with a reduction in chairs reported the following experiences. In the first instance they all found it impossible to avoid times when their entire teaching group were sitting on chairs. Sometimes this arose through the teacher's own decision; at other times it arose through the actions of the children. Although the frequency of these occasions was rare and their duration short-lived, the teachers regarded them as an essential part of their work. In so far as these experiences served educational purposes that could not be achieved in any other way, the teachers were unwilling to abandon them for the sake of a handful of chairs.

A second experience related to the use of chairs as a movable resource. The teachers conceded that it might be possible to use less than 100 per cent chairs for much of the school day but had found that this usually required a certain proportion of chairs to be moved constantly from place to place. This occurred, for example, when a group of children wanted to set up a 'school' in the 'shop', or a 'hairdressing salon' in the home-base. The teachers not only felt that the movement of chairs created avoidable disruption but also that the initial shortage of chairs had an inhibiting effect on their pupils' freedom of choice.

A third observation (made by the teachers of younger children) was that a limited supply of chairs could interfere with the educational principle that certain well-used areas (eg, milk, sewing, library) should retain a fixed allocation of chairs. The justification for this policy was that the presence of chairs could help children to perform activities that might otherwise be too difficult. It was also argued in favour of such a policy that it helped to prevent certain practical problems (eg, spillage of milk, loss of sewing needles, damage of books). In these instances the combined weight of the educational and administrative advantages was sufficient to convince the teachers of the need for extra chairs.

Finally, all the teachers reported that they were unwilling to allow children to write while standing at a work surface or lying on the floor. Out of the spin-offs from the general debate about seating levels has been the suggestions that children should be allowed to write in an upright or prone position. Without exception, the case-study teachers reacted unfavourably to this idea. Like the erstwhile master of St Andrews Grammar School, they felt that children who are learning to write should be encouraged to use a suitable surface and a comfortable chair.

Conclusion

This essay considers a rather curious discrepancy between theory and practice. It focuses on a school of thought which holds that a modern primary school can be adequately equipped with less than one chair per child. By examining the consequences of such a strategy it questions the practice whereby chairs become a shared rather than a guaranteed resource. The fact that chairs are to be shared means that they are downgraded to the same status as painting easels, water tanks and sand trays. As a result, special rules are needed to regulate the pupils' access to them. In turn, these rules have an impact on the type of methods and curricula which can be used by teachers.

For instance, one of the case-study teachers reported that a provision of 66 per cent chairs in her previous school had not only created a clearly visible three-ring circus within each teaching area but had also ossified the pupil composition of each group. As indicated elsewhere in these essays the difference between group and personalised teaching is rather more than a matter of teacher choice.

Sources

Apart from the sources quoted in footnotes, there is very little written on the subject. Thus, most of the information in this essay comes from discussions with the case-study teachers and other researchers, and from material provided by a furniture consultant and an architect.

6

ALL WORK AND NO PLAY?

> "*Learning experiences, in so far as they are a school responsibility are structured. . . . They are arranged according to more or less definite views about learning processes, about general human development, about the expectations of various groups external to the school, and about what is feasible and desirable in an institutional setting where many constraints limit the realisation of the values to which educators aspire*'.
>
> (Malcolm Skilbeck, *Educationalist*)[1]

The labels 'work' and 'play' are commonly used to differentiate the various activities of the primary school. This essay highlights the changing use of these terms by analysing the views of a small group of teachers who wanted to abolish such a distinction. Overall, it suggests that debates about work and play are not so much about differentiating the curriculum as about changing it.

One of the basic distinctions in primary education is between 'work' and 'play'. The former has connotations of intellectual growth, industry and public achievement whereas latter usually expresses ideas about social development, recreation, and fulfilment. In turn, work is sometimes considered central to the

---

[1] In P H Taylor and J Walton (editors), *The Curriculum: Research, Innovation, and Change* (London: Ward Lock Educational, 1973), pp 116-7.

primary school curriculum whereas play is treated as a more marginal activity, optional rather than essential.

This distinction between work and play is prominent in many contemporary discussions about early education. Basically, there are two (longstanding) schools of thought. One view—sometimes associated with the name of Friedrich Frobel—is that the early school curriculum should provide for and build upon the spontaneous play of young children. The alternative position—sometimes associated with the name of Maria Montessori—is that the early school curriculum should, from the outset, be organised around a much more interventionist type of teaching. At the risk of over-simplification, the Froebelian view is that work is a special kind of play whereas the Montessorian position is that play is a special kind of work.

In recent years the increase of pre-schooling has given these debates a new lease of life. Thus, *play groups* reflect the Froebelian view whereas nursery *schools* tend to embody the ideas of Montessori. The distinction between work and play can also be used to characterise the difference between pre-schooling and primary schooling. The former emphasises the educational value of play, the latter stresses the importance of work.

These views about work and play were also reproduced among the teachers in the case-study school. In particular, a small group —the starting point of this essay—took up an extreme position and argued against any kind of work/play distinction. For instance, during the course of an interview one teacher prefaced certain remarks by: 'When I say water play, I mean water work'. On a different occasion another teacher argued that all references to 'play' in a description of her teaching should, in the final version, be replaced with the word 'work'. In short, this group of teachers aimed to overcome the arbitrary nature of the work/play distinction by labelling all activities as 'work', irrespective of their content or purpose.

At first glance this issue appears to be a personal matter. If a teacher decides to regard certain activities as work rather than play (or so it seems) her action need be of little concern to other people. However, in certain respects this relabelling activity had a much wider impact. To remain true to their beliefs, the work-not-play teachers also tried to modify their classroom language. For example, children would be asked if they wished to 'work' in the painting area or in the 'house'. This public demonstration by the work-not-play teachers inevitably brought their views to the notice of other teachers, pupils and parents. In this way the work-not-play debate became a social rather than a personal issue. And, as described below, it created all kinds of new problems.

ATTITUDES AND PRACTICES

Beliefs about work and play are not only expressed verbally during informal discussions and staff meetings but also actively in the day to day organisation of teaching. Basically, the work-not-play teachers tried to implement two related assumptions:
1. That the same degree of seriousness should be accorded every aspect of the school day.
2. That every school activity should be regarded as contributing to a child's education in some way or another.

In practice the first assumption was particularly difficult to demonstrate. For instance, to treat every activity with equal seriousness does not necessarily mean that each one should receive the same amount of a teacher's (or pupil's) time. Neither does it mean that each activity should take place with equal frequency. As these illustrations suggest, seriousness is a difficult attribute to display.

The second viewpoint could be demonstrated more visibly. It became manifest when teachers combined 'work' and 'play' activities (eg, painting number patterns) or when they gave greater priority to activities that conventionally take place later in the day (ie, after 'work'). Some teachers, for instance, included 'milk' as part of their pupils' daily *work* schedules. Similarly, other teachers read to their pupils in the middle of the day rather than at the end; or encouraged the children to use the 'wet' (ie, play) areas, before they started their 'dry' (ie, work) activities.

To this limited extent the work-not-play teachers were able to reorganise their teaching around a weakened distinction between work and play. In other respects, however, they were less successful. One minor problem was that the teachers often found it linguistically clumsy to replace 'play' by 'work'. Games, for example, are still conventionally 'played' not 'worked'. Likewise, 'play' is still the most acceptable antonym for 'work'. (If children are not working, what are they doing?)

A more deep-rooted and delicate source of difficulty for the teachers related to their pupils' views about work and play. By the time children reach the age of five most of them already have well-established ideas about such activities (eg, sandpits are for play, books are for work). Thus, by abandoning the notion of 'play', the case-study teachers were quite aware that their resultant behaviour might conflict with the pupils' expectations. Worse still, they realised that their actions might be interpreted as a deliberate attempt to counteract the values held by the parents of their children. Thus, albeit unwittingly, the teacher's efforts to dissolve the boundaries between work and play became a potential source of confusion at school and at home.

Despite these practical and ethical problems, the work-not-play teachers were reluctant to abandon their viewpoint. To a variable degree, they continued to use 'work' instead of 'play' in their discussions with the children. Overall, however, they accepted that the countervailing strength of outside opinion was, at least in the short term, probably far greater than their own.

THE VIEWS OF THE PUPILS

During the course of the research an attempt was made to put these ideas in context by looking more closely at the views of the pupils. A random sample of five children from each of the five classes in primary one, two and three (ie, a total of seventy-five children), were asked six questions about their school activities:

1. Where do you have your milk?
2. When do you have your milk?
3. What sort of things do you do in the courtyard?
4. What do you do when you've finished your assignment?
5. When do you usually paint?
6. Who usually decides what you paint?

The expectancy—based on earlier observation and discussion—was that the responses of the older children would reflect a strengthening rather than a weakening of the work/play distinction and that, in part, this would result from a gradual differentiation of space and time into areas and units of work and play. For instance, it was anticipated that a higher proportion of primary three children would:
a. Drink their milk outside the class (ie, work) area.
b. Take milk at break (ie, play time) rather than at other times of the day.
c. Work inside the building rather than outside in the courtyards.

Although the interviews showed considerable variation from class to class, the overall expectation was sustained. The responses were as follows:

	Primary One	*Primary Three*
Children who reported drinking their milk outside the class areas	0%	100%
Children who used the words 'break' or 'playtime' to describe their milk time	8%	43%
Children who reported that they had *not* been out into the courtyards during the previous term	38%	64%

A related observation in the case study school was that a greater part of the primary three day was devoted to activities deemed to be 'work'. In these classes 'work' had begun to take greater prominence in the daily programme of work. The interviews reinforced this observation. When asked "What do you do when you've finished your assignment/jobs?", the replies from primary one more frequently contained the word 'play' than those from primary three children (39 per cent as against 22 per cent).

Specifically, the primary three children usually referred to other curriculum activities. For example, 40 per cent of their replies contained the words 'painting' and/or 'drawing' (compared with 4 per cent of the replies in primary one). At first glance painting and drawing—especially if they are optional and pupil-directed—might seem to be synonymous with play. However, in the case-study school this did not appear to be true. By the time the children had reached primary three, craft work began to fill a specific slot in the day and in most cases was organised around topics outlined by the class teacher. Again, these overall differences between primary one and three were reflected in the way the children answered the interview questions. For example, more primary three children reported that they did painting at a special time or after their 'work':

When do you usually paint?

	Primary One	Primary Three
Special time (eg, 'after lunch')	16%	20%
Any time	20%	4%
After 'work'	20%	48%
(none of these)	44%	28%

Similarly, more primary three children reported that their teacher decided what they should paint:

Who usually decides what you paint?

	Primary One	Primary Two	Primary Three
Me	56%	24%	32%
The teacher	12%	16%	44%
Both (me or the teacher)	4%	40%	16%
(none of these)	28%	20%	8%

These pupil references suggest that in the period between primary one and primary three painting shifts across the school curriculum from being a play activity to being a work activity. The interviews provide further support for this idea. In so far as the largest group of primary two children gave both 'Me' and the 'teacher' as the source of decisions about painting, their replies come somewhere between the contrasting patterns of primary one and primary three.

DISCUSSION

The first part of this essay distinguishes the concepts of work and play as used in the primary school. In particular, it focuses upon a small group of teachers in the case-study school who sought to abolish the work/play distinction. In many respects this work-not-play group were the leading edge of a more general trend within the school (and, possibly, in primary education). However, what made them particularly conspicuous was not so much their classroom practice as their classroom language.

The second part of this essay considers the concepts of work and play from the point of view of the pupils in the case-study school. Contrary to the (short-term) hopes of work-not-play teachers, it suggests that there was a hardening of the distinction between work and play over the age range from primary one to primary three. Although the school day was increasingly dominated by activities labelled as 'work', this did not arise from the breaking down of barriers as from the gradually withering away of those activities which, lower down the school, were conventionally defined as play. In the case study instance some of the earlier activities (eg, painting) were incorporated into the working day whereas others (eg, use of the courtyards) progressively disappeared from the curriculum (or were relegated to the status of out-of-school activities). The fact that the primary three day was more work-orientated than the primary one day reflected a change in the curriculum, not a change in the labelling practices used by the teachers.

In the widest sense, debates about work and play in the primary school are not only about a search for a suitable terminology but also about a search for a suitable curriculum.

7

EPISODES OF SCHOOL LIFE

"This open-plan school is more structured than I imagined."

(Parent)

This essay is primarily informative. Three descriptive snapshots one from each of the first three years—try to capture the complexity and continuity of life in a modern primary school. As in First Days at School, **each account is followed by a brief explanatory comment.**

(1) A DAY IN THE LIFE OF A PUPIL

Ian Rae has spent almost a year at school and is approaching his sixth birthday. Compared with the other boys in his class he is slightly smaller in body weight and height. His most obvious identifying features are a round freckled face and light ginger hair. On the day in question (13th May 1975) he gets up soon after 7am, puts on his school uniform and tidies his room. While Mr Rae takes his younger brother to spend the day with Granny, Ian polishes off the breakfast prepared by his mother. At 8.20 Morag and her father arrive to take Ian to school. En route they collect Mary, who is also in Ian's class.

08.50 By the time Ian enters the school playground most of the twenty-four children in his class have already hung up their coats and emptied their school bags into the drawers that serve in place of desks. Ian comes straight into the learning area but before he takes off his jacket is attracted by Peter's red-uniformed 'action man'. Ian returns to the lobby, hangs up his coat, unpacks his briefcase, and then rejoins Peter to talk about the action man.

08.58	Without prompting Ian is the first to line up for assembly. He holds the door open for the remainder of the class to file through to the hall.
09.11	After a short biblical story, two prayers, and a hymn, the children return to their class base. As usual they sit on the floor around Miss Dean's chair. She asks them for their 'news'. Although Ian is at the front and puts his hand up immediately, he has to wait while Miss Dean gives other children the opportunity to speak. Eventually Ian is given his chance. "I was out in the garden. I thought it would be awfully long while I waited for Mummy. We went shopping. Some for Mummy, some for me (pause) and we left some for Daddy. For the rest of the news time Ian sits silently except when drawn into Alan's account ("Ian, you know where I live . . .").
09.28	Miss Dean reminds the children not to forget their milk and then gives out two sets of jotters and the newly marked workbooks.
09.30	Ian takes his books and sits near the blackboard at a small table with Maurice, Iris and Janet. As a class exercise Miss Dean dictates a set of words which the children write in their 'sounds' jotter. ("wish . . . I made a *wish*." dish, crash, splash, rash, shelf, sheets, ships, shells, shops.)
09.33	Before leaving the class to work on their own, Miss Dean indicates the layout to be used in the sums book, and rehearses the individual work on sounds. ("What is a mat*ch*? . . . What is a *ch*imp? . . . What does this word say?") The blackboard already lists the programme of work ('(1) sums (2) sounds (3) workbook (4) choosing') and, to one side, indicates the supplementary material for certain of the tasks. The children can complete the work programme in any order they wish.
09.44	Ian gets up, goes over to his drawer and puts his workbook away. Then, apparently changing his mind, puts the sounds book away and retrieves his workbook. (The workbook contains printed exercises which require the children to fill in words—in this case 'eye', 'ear' and 'nose'—and then use them in a variety of contexts. Each child is expected to do at least one page.) Ian makes a mistake (writes 'nose' on a diagram of the face instead of 'ear'). He fetches an eraser from the

	side table and makes the correction. Puts 'nose' in the box for 'ear'. Fetches the eraser again.
09.51	Ian reads the sentences aloud sounding out the key word: "This one has no e..a..r..s./This one has one eye./This one has no nose." He delves into the two tins of coloured pencils on the table to colour in the face.
10.00	Ian has reached second page of workbook. A mild dispute breaks out between Maurice and Iris as to which coloured pencils they should be using. Ian seems unaware of this discussion but eventually breaks in to tell them "You two use these pencils, and we'll use these".
10.02	Ian won't let Iris use his six-inch ruler. Iris asks again. Ian refuses but adds a reason: "It's a new one". (The children are free to use the class rulers which are kept along with the erasers.)
10.05	Ian turns to a new page in his workbook but decides not to continue. He puts his ruler in the leather pencil case and places his chair neatly under the table. He shows his workbook to Miss Dean before putting it on the pile for marking. He goes over to Peter and Moira who are playing on the floor with wooden blocks and the action man. Ian seems more attracted by the latter, especially when Peter indicates that it can talk.
10.14	Ian retains the action man while the other two build a fortress out of the blocks. He tells them to "sshh" when they make a noise turning over the blocks in the storage tray.
10.18	Miss Dean joins the trio to talk about the action man and the fortress. Before leaving the group she announces break to the whole class by reminding them to be ready to come back early for P.E.
10.20	(Morning break.) Ian spends most of the time chasing about the playground with four classmates. Occasionally he gets a little perturbed when they become over-boisterous.
10.43	The class line up at the edge of the playground while the remaining 250 children continue their playtime. Mrs Lee (the auxiliary) marshalls them into school. The P.E. teacher, Mrs Aire, is waiting for them in the hall. The children take off their shoes and socks and spend 20 minutes on various running, stretching, curling and jumping activities. Like the rest of the class Ian partici-

EPISODES OF SCHOOL LIFE

pates fully in the spirit of the occasion ("Jump up like a rocket taking off").

11.05 Ian puts on his sandals and is fourth in the line waiting to leave the hall. He chats with his neighbour. Since the music 'room' is in use, the class return by going the long way round through four other teaching areas.

11.08 Ian sits with three others at the milk table. Their discussion is interrupted when Mr Hamilton asks them about their morning activities.

11.23 Upon a request from the teacher, Ian fetches his Ladybird reading book and sits with Jane and Iris round Miss Dean's chair. They take it in turn to read from prose passages and word lists.

11.30 Ian puts his reading book away and goes over to the other side of the class area to join a boy playing with a plastic interlocking construction kit. After a few seconds he changes his mind and walks through Mrs Barber's area out to the toilet in the lobby.

11.32 On his return Ian talks briefly with the boy using the construction kit. He then fetches his pencil case and sum book. On a fresh squared page he copies two number lines (0 1 2...9) and the first column of eight sums from the blackboard. (At this point Ian cannot refer to his teacher since she has briefly disappeared from the teaching area.) He begins to fill in the answers: $8 + = 8$; $6 + = 8$; etc.

11.37 Ian gets up to fetch an eraser but realises that Maurice already has one. Another boy comes by, also searching for an eraser. Maurice asks Ian for help with his sounds work. Ian suggests he should think of the sounds: "*Ch*, it's got a *ch* in it".

11.46 Ian takes 3 Cuisenaire rods from the tray left on the table by Iris but makes very little apparent use of them. He begins to write out the second column of sums (eg, $7 + = 8$; $1 + = 8$). While talking to himself about the work: "I wish it's finished" . . . (later) Oh dear".

11.57 Ian rubs out the second answer column of 8s and writes them in again. (By this time some children have completed their set work and begun to do 'choosing'.)

12.01 On completing the sums Ian takes his book for Miss Dean's inspection. He then replaces it in his drawer but remembers that it should have been put on the marking pile. He starts work in his 'sounds' book. (Although the jotter comprises blank pages, Miss Dean has already inserted suitable guidelines on a blank double page.) The right hand page is divided into six squares and Ian begins to prepare a picture to illustrate the word 'catch'. He fills the entire square with colouring and then remembers he has left out the word. While Ian attempts to rub out some of the colour, Iris asks him for words beginning with 'st'.

12.19 Ian fills all six squares (catch, match, stitch, witch, pitch, rich) and then begins to write his sentences on the bottom half of the left-hand page. The key words are on the blackboard.
"I see a *cheek*.
I see a *chimp*.
I liek *cheese*.
I *choose* at scool not always."
He carefully enters all the full stops as a final flourish.

12.22 Ian begins to make up words and put them against the numbers on the top half of the same page.

sh	*st*	*ch*
(1) shot	(4) star	(7) choose
(2) ship	(5) still	(8) chat
(3) shop	(6) stick	(9) chose

12.25 Ian puts his book to be marked, watches girls playing at 'hymns' in the base, and then moves on to dismantle some unifix blocks.

12.33 Ian starts to play football on the floor with another boy using pieces of modelling apparatus.

12.35 Miss Dean asks the class to tidy up and then gather round her chair for 'stories'. Maurice has brought a sub-aqua diver's wrist compass. Miss Dean uses this opportunity to give a short object lesson: "Who would use this watch? . . . What else does a diver wear?" Ian answers three of her questions ("I know why they've got flippers—to help them swim.")

12.45 Ian listens while Miss Dean asks the class riddles from a book brought in by one of the girls. (Eg, why does a cook put on a white hat? To cover his head.)

12.55 The entire class are sent to fetch their coats and

school bags. (Although there is no homework, the children take their reading books home.)

13.00 The class gather round their teacher to say a formal and unison "Good morning, Miss Dean". Ian disappears immediately to go home for his dinner and a haircut.

As the last children gradually melt away the school cleaners began to appear with their vacuum cleaners, brushes and rubbish bags. Only 37 days remain until the summer holidays.

Commentary

In the context of these essays the pattern of Ian's day is noteworthy for the following reasons. First it gives some indication of the personalised/individualised form of teaching used by Miss Dean. Ian spends only a small part of the day as part of a teaching group. Second, it reveals that Ian does not follow the work schedule as indicated on the blackboard but, rather, chooses his own sequence of activities. Third, the account records the wealth of educational interaction that occurs between the children—even though they are rarely working on the same activity. Fourth, it suggests that there are relatively few contacts between Ian's class and those in the neighbouring areas. Finally, the pattern of events demonstrates that by the third term of the school year the children in the case-study school have internalised much of the daily and weekly routine. In many cases they initiate specific activities even before they are requested by their teachers.

(2) A DAY IN THE LIFE OF A TEACHER

Although this is her first year in the open-plan annexe, Miss Law has been with the school for four years. On Thursday, 15th May—just like any other working day—she arrives in school before 08.30 and goes straight to her work area and begins writing the day's programme on the blackboard. As she writes, the space becomes filled with a set of eight sums; work for the children's busy books; and a summary of the basic tasks of the day ('(1) red sum book, (2) busy book, (3) four sentences, (4) paint a landing craft'). Much of the work is planned round the theme of 'space exploration'. The children's ages range from six to seven years.

08.40 Three of the class are already standing around

	themselves. Mrs Michie (an auxiliary) is topping up the painting jars with fresh paint. Miss Law goes to the staffroom for a quick cup of coffee.
08.50	She returns and talks informally with Mr Hamilton and some of the children. There is a build-up of children in the class area. Some of the boys are playing in the space rocket.
09.00	Miss Law asks Hugh to round up the rest of the class from the playground. (There are no school bells.) The children (11 girls and 14 boys) line up in the class area and file into the hall for the primary two hymn practice. Five other teachers leave their children in Miss Law's care. 140 children sit round the piano while she rehearses certain difficult passages and checks that the children can match the tune to the words.
09.08	Mrs Nuthall comes into the hall and briefly changes place with Miss Law. She was not satisfied with the children's singing at the previous assembly and asks them to try the hymn again.
09.12	Miss Law returns to the piano and rehearses each of the six classes in turn. As some of the non-participating children become restless, Miss Law stops the practice to remind them of the disturbance they are creating.
09.24	The practice is brought to a close with all the children singing the first verse of the hymn. The children file out row by row. Upon returning to her class Miss Law asks the children to bring their homework books and join her in the class base. First, she tells them that she is postponing 'news' until the end of the day. Then, one by one, five different children are asked to read what they have written about 'a spacecraft landing on earth'. The whole group is invited to comment on the answers. The discussion leads to a minor diversion when the children consider the relationship between heat and friction. Miss Law asks the children to rub their hands together.
09.35	Miss Law moves on to the homework sums and, with the children's assistance, recalculates the answers. When asked, three children indicate that they made an error. Miss Law comments on their answers by asking, for instance, whether they have the right number in the 'hundreds' column.
09.37	The work programme is outlined. (Because of lack

of space on the blackboard, Miss Law is unable to write out the vocabulary words until the children have entered the sums into their books. This they must do some time before break.) As the children leave the base they put their homework jotters to be marked, fetch their sum books from the drawers, and sit at the tables in the class area. While she moves around checking that everyone has a pencil, Miss Law reminds the class to write the date and their practice numbers before starting to write down the sums. After helping a boy look for a lead pencil among a jar of coloured pencils, she waits while the class write out the first sum; and then goes through the process with them.

09.49 While leaving the children to continue with the sums or to move on to another activity, Miss Law consults her mark book and then calls out the names of one of the reading groups. Four boys bring their books to where she is sitting. The boys read individually as Miss Law continuously scans the rest of the class. Occasionally she intervenes to elicit information, to prompt, or to encourage.

09.58 Miss Law gives Neil permission to go out to the lobby. The reading group is disbanded. Neil returns with a painting overall but is unable to find paper in the painting area. He appeals to Miss Law for help. Miss Law goes over to the painting area and finds some paper. She reminds the class to complete their busy books and sum books before break. Sally and Martin are asked to bring out their reading books.

10.06 Miss Law explains to the class that they must finish writing out the sums so that she can clean the board during break.

10.10 End of second reading group. Miss Law asks the 'milk boys' to fetch the crate and straws from the lobby. She asks Simon to bring his reading book and reminds Hugh to copy down all the sums.

10.15 Miss Law begins marking the homework books while the children drink their milk. The front table are exhorted to finish their sums. Miss Law reminds the children to come suitably dressed the following week for the school photograph.

10.24 When the children go out to the playground, Miss Law discovers that Hugh has not written out all the sums. She marks the rest of the homework books over coffee in the staffroom while chatting with colleagues. Their discussion centres on the mechanics of teaching arithmetic addition.

11.00 The class reassembles after break. Miss Law asks the four children who have returned to their painting to leave what they are doing. All the children are requested to fetch their 'sounds' books. Miss Law stands at the blackboard and writes up the 28 special words offered by the children (moon, crater, rockets . . . capsule, spacewalk). Some words provoke discussion. (Eg, is 'astronaut' preferable to 'spaceman'?)

11.15 Miss Law asks the children to choose four of the words and write a sentence for each. Some children return to their painting (and leave the sentences until later). Miss Law sits down and begins to mark the sum books. Two boys interrupt her carrying a long thin painting of a space rocket. She discusses with them where it might be displayed. Eventually she climbs on a stool to hang it in the open space between the class and painting areas.

11.25 When Miss Law returns to marking, the children come out to collect their books. If there are any errors the children correct them and return them to be checked.

11.27 The 'phone rings persistently in the lobby. Miss Law rushes out to answer it. She returns and speaks to Hugh who is still working at his sums. Tricia asks to go to the toilet. Mrs Mackinnon, one of the other teachers, stops by to speak to Miss Law. Two boys ask to go to the Library. The marking continues.

11.40 Miss Law finishes marking the available sum books and then moves around the class to visit the children who are still working at the tables. While sorting out some sticky paper beside the storage shelves, Miss Law overhears a girl asking for the spelling of 'engine'.

11.50 The class is reminded that there is only 10 minutes left to finish their books. Miss Law cuts out sticky paper while helping Hugh with his sums —by now he has resorted to unifix blocks.

11.58 Miss Law asks the boys who played in the rocket

to remember to give other children a turn on subsequent occasions. A boy brings out a broken biro.

12.00 All the class are sitting at their tables. Different children give out scissors, sticky paper, and thin card. Miss Law shows the entire class how to make a rocket by folding, cutting, and mounting the sticky paper. Hugh continues with his sentences. Miss Law helps the children who have cut incorrectly.

12.20 The children decorate their cut-outs as they wish. Some use scraps of sticky paper, others use coloured pencils. One boy asks if he can include the American flag. Miss Law finds one for him in a class library book.

12.27 The children who gave out the equipment are asked to collect it in again. Miss Law writes the homework on the blackboard (six spelling words, three sentences, and two 3-digit subtraction sums). She gives out the homework jotters. One girl asks for a new book.

12.41 Some children begin to pack up their school bags and go into the base. Miss Law chats informally with them while waiting for the others. (Two are at the toilet, five are writing out the homework.)

12.45 Miss Law starts the 'news' session. Individual children stand up and recount such activities as visiting the dentist or staying at grandma's. Others have brought books on space travel to show the rest of the class. These activities spill over into the time Miss Law normally sets aside for reading a story to the children.

12.57 Miss Law dismisses the class from the base and reminds the milk boys to carry out the crate. She talks with another teacher while the children put on their coats.

After lunch Miss Law supervises a primary three class in the school library from 1.30 until two o'clock. (This is part of her duty as school librarian.) During the rest of the afternoon she completes her marking and clears up the few items of debris that remain scattered around the class area. Although Miss Law leaves behind the hurly-burly of class work when she goes home at three o'clock, the school day is still not over. During the evening she sets aside a few quiet minutes to consider the day's events and to write out her work plan for the following day.

Commentary

Miss Law's teaching day provides data on the conduct of teaching and learning in a modern primary school. Her re-scheduling of the 'news' period pin-points the fact that teaching in an open-plan school is as much about the manipulation of time as it is about the management of space. Unlike Ian and his classmates (see *A Day in the Life of a Pupil*) Miss Law's children follow the day much more as a group. As a result, the periods of individual work fit a little less easily into the overall pattern. This is partly because the children are not always free to leave what they are doing and join a group or class activity. The fact that Miss Law is a primary two teacher is also reflected in the increased literacy component in her work programme. For instance, she is able to monitor the children's progress through marking their books as well as through observing them at work or listening to what they have to say. The increased literacy of the curriculum and teaching methods also means that the children are seated for a greater part of the day. As a consequence Miss Law moves more freely around the area. In general the primary one teachers in the case-study school remained relatively stationary while the children moved about. In primary two and three the teachers became more mobile, the children more sedentary.

(3) A DAY IN THE LIFE OF A CLASS

3M comprise 30 boys and girls whose ages cluster around eight years. Their rectangular class area (designed for 25 children) opens out on to a 'wet' zone that is shared with two other classes. On Tuesday, 20th May 1975, the children begin to arrive in the school building by 08.30. When John comes in carrying a bucket of winkles, the other children gather round. He takes some out of the bucket and claims that "they might attack the school". The other children seem both horrified and amused.

08.50   Mrs Thomson enters the class area. Immediately the children focus their attention on her presence. After counting the class while they sit at their tables, she asks them to gather round her chair by the blackboard. Most of the children sit on the floor.

EPISODES OF SCHOOL LIFE

08.56   The last child arrives. For the next 30 minutes the class eagerly confront their teacher with photo money and with the excitement of their weekend's exploits. (Many of the children have been away from home since Monday has been a local holiday.) Mysterious plastic bags are unpacked to reveal sea shells, foreign coins, holiday leaflets, and other objects for the display areas. Gavin has brought a model windmill. Other children describe their holiday activities—a visit from granny, a joyride in an aeroplane, a shopping expedition, a weekend in a caravan. In their anxiety to catch the teacher's eye, some children forget what they are going to say. When Mrs Thomson asks if any one has had a 'bad' weekend, only Gordon replies in the affirmative.

09.25   Although not all the children had been given the opportunity to contribute their news, Mrs Thomson directs the class's attention to the work already on the blackboard. (Since about half the class are to go to craftwork in the afternoon, she feels under some pressure to give them the maximum time to complete their formal activities.)

09.37   The children disperse to their desks while the jotters are given out. Without any apparent sign, six boys move into the painting area and continue their co-operative art work (preparing a life-size portrait of a viking warrior, and a scaled-down painting of a longship). The remainder of the class begin the work programme. Not all of them start with the first item. Mrs Thomson reminds those who have 'see me' in their books to join her in the reading area. Three children come forward. Stephen asks to go to the toilet.

09.45   The 'blue' reading group (two boys, two girls) are requested to bring their books to the reading area. While the children are reading aloud, Mrs Thomson maintains contact with the rest of the class. One girl comes out for a spelling word; another brings a note from her parents. Hamish asks for the pink paint. After some discussion about possible alternative procedures, Mrs Thomson asks him to wait until Mrs Anderson (the auxiliary) becomes available.

10.00   End of first reading group. Donald gains Mrs Thomson's attention and sits opposite her on the reading bench to give her his 'news'. Jean takes her maths book to be marked. Susan has broken the buckle on her shoe; Mrs Thomson offers to 'phone her mother to bring a replacement at hometime. Different children ask for spelling words—ocean, telephone. One of the painting group asks for white sticky paper to make the horns in the viking's helmet. Susan is sent to the nurse for a pin to fix her shoe.

10.15   Julie receives a reminder that she "hasn't done a thing since last time." All the children are now sitting at the tables. (Although not conventional desks, the tables have a shelf below the working surface on which the children can keep their personal belongings. Their school bags are slung on the backs of the chairs.)

10.20   As it is raining, Mrs Thomson cautions the children to take care while they are in school during playtime. Within two minutes the whole class have migrated into the wet area to eat their sweets, crisps, apples and sandwiches. During playtime they gradually drift back into the class area and stand around chatting.

10.55   After break Mrs Thomson gives the entire class a short spelling exercise based on the previous day's homework (stayed, clever, drove, home, next). She puts the new homework on the blackboard for the children to write in their homework notebooks. (It is linked to the class work and includes six spelling words and four simple division sums.) The other activities continue. Someone asks "What colour is an octopus?"

The yellow reading group convene (five members). Two boys go out of the class area to paint.

11.15   Some children begin to finish their work programme and move on to optional activities (painting, plasticine, 'My book on the vikings'). Some children take longer at their formal tasks since they have additional work specially devised by Mrs Thomson.

11.25   Children move between the tables ("Can I borrow your felt pen?"). Gordon and Julie are searching for an eraser on the floor. Children approach Mrs Thomson with a range of problems (difficulties with spelling and maths, requests for the large scissors). While answering their inquiries she moves around among the pupils' tables tackling problems as they arise. Richard asks for help with spelling 'fiddlesticks' and 'bottle'. Other children are looking at items in the display areas (one each for 'the sea', 'Holland', and 'the vikings'). Four children are modelling in plasticine.

11.50 Julie receives some individual tuition. Mrs Thomson stands near her while marking work brought by other children. Some of them receive special encouragement to complete the work before they go to knitting.

11.58 Two girls begin to line up at the edge of the carpeted class area. Eventually, all the class are ready for lunch. Some go off to the hall while the others remain to eat their packed lunches in the wet area. The weather begins to improve and by 12.30 most of the children have moved out into the playground.

13.05 The class reassembles and sit at their tables. Mrs Thomson sends the knitters out into the wet area. Mrs Robertson (the craft teacher) arrives as they are unpacking their knitting bags. Under her supervision the group rapidly settle to their task of knitting small garments for soft toys. They continue with this activity until 14.25.

13.07 The purple reading group assemble in the reading area. Martin asks permission to go to the Library. Julie complains that she is not feeling well. Only six children remain working at the tables. Scott searches for his orange pencil. Mrs Thomson catches his eye while listening to the reading group.

13.27 Julie approaches Mrs Thomson and is asked to sit beside her. Mrs Thomson marks Julie's books. Jonathan asks to go to the toilet. Two girls come back from the Library. Julie gets up to sharpen her pencil and returns to her seat. The reading group move on to a new story. Mrs Thomson discusses it with them in relative peace. End of reading group.

13.40 A girl starts work in plasticine. Gordon is drawing a windmill. Julie completes the work programme with Mrs Thomson's assistance.

14.00 Two boys prepare a collage to decorate the sails of the long ship. Mrs Thomson convenes a 'poetry' corner. Eight children gather—some with

	their own poems. They take it in turns to read aloud.
1405	Julie sorts out the jotters into neat piles. Kevin cleans some paint off his jacket. Katie colours a chart of wild flowers. Only five children are sitting at the tables.
14.15	Mrs Thomson invites the two boys who appear to be wandering about to join the poetry group. Other children are listening to the poems although they are not officially part of the poetry group.
14.28	Paul asks Mrs Thomson to inspect his plasticine model. Some children begin to pack their school bags. The knitters return.

At 14.35 the class listen while Mrs Thomson announces that she will be absent the following day. She also reminds them that it will be the last day for the photo money. When the children are ready and standing by their tables, they reply as a group to Mrs Thomson's "Good afternoon". The 'party' people are dismissed first (it is Heather's birthday). By 14.40 the children have all disappeared leaving Mrs Thomson to complete her marking and write out the next day's work on the blackboard.

Commentary

By the time the children in the case-study school reach primary three their day takes on new features. It is longer (there is a 95-minute session after lunch) and more subject to the rigours of external timetabling (dictated, in part, by the greater use of specialist teachers). At the same time, the pupils' physical growth and the consequent use of larger chairs and tables reduces the amount of circulation space in the teaching area. A third (and related) feature of the day is that pupil circulation is also reduced by the introduction of tables with built-in storage space. This last innovation—prompted by the growing volume of printed material used by the children—also means that every child has a specific work place and his 'own' seat. Finally, the increased use of blackboard resources also presupposes that the tables and chairs can be arranged so that each child can see the board.

Taken separately, organisational factors such as these are

relatively trivial; taken together, they exert a considerable influence on the daily work of teachers and pupils.

* * * *

Note

These three accounts were prepared to give some idea of the pattern of life within an open-plan school. A class, a pupil and a teacher were selected at random from the population of the case-study school. The only restriction placed upon the selection process was that the final sample should include one representative from each year. The class teachers were given at least a day's advance notice of the observation. It was explained that the purpose of the data collection was to prepare an account that would be comprehensible to an interested outsider. Within a few days of each observation, the teachers were provided with a preliminary draft to comment upon. In two cases a further draft was submitted.

8

THE LOGIC OF THE OPEN-PLAN SCHOOL

"Knowledge one has acquired without sufficient structure to tie it together is knowledge that is likely to be forgotten."

(Jerome Bruner, *Psychologist*)[1]

This final essay returns to the basic question posed in Chapter 1. It reconsiders the concept of open-ness as used in architecture and education. Its main purpose is to integrate these ideas within the changing assumptions, patterns and priorities of primary schooling. Central to the argument is that new curricula require new teaching methods; and that new teaching methods require new or reallocated resources of equipment, time, and human endeavour.

It is a truism of education that the daily lives of teachers and pupils are affected by the political, economic, and intellectual climate of a nation. The extent of this influence, however, is less well understood. It is very difficult to translate national statistics into the day-to-day realities of the classroom. Very little is known about the real or potential impact of, for example, variations in pupil-teacher ratios, changes in school design, modifications in the length of the school day, or alterations in the duration of compulsory schooling.

In traditional 'scientific' research terms these questions have proved unanswerable; even when all the relevant variables are identifiable, the problem of untangling their relative effects

---

[1] J Bruner, *The Process of Education* (Cambridge, Mass.: Harvard University Press, 1960), p 31.

remains intractable. Nevertheless, questions of the form: *What are the conditions necessary for the translation of an untried idea into the realm of educational practice?* are still central to any consideration of educational change.

Clearly, this issue lies at the heart of discussions about primary education. For more than two decades architects, administrators, educationists, and teachers have jostled with each other to present their own specialist viewpoints. In turn, ideas about space utilisation, cost efficiency, learning effectiveness, and job satisfaction have reverberated through the many layers of the school system.

This essay attempts to explain these developments by drawing out some of the more crucial ideas, events and practices. Overall, it retains an historical perspective: the open plan school is not an isolated entity but merely one of the more visible manifestations of a much broader movement affecting secondary as well as primary education.

OUTSIDE EVENTS AND IDEAS

As outlined in earlier essays, the open-plan school attempts to provide for a particular constellation of educational assumptions and practices. In themselves, of course, these ideas are nothing new; their presence has been recorded on the educational agenda for many years. Their rise to prominence, therefore, requires a different explanation. The argument of this essay is that a separate set of historical and demographic factors has enabled them to take root and develop. What are these outside factors?

One major influence on the nature of primary schooling relates to the gradual raising of the school leaving age. Whenever the duration of compulsory schooling is increased, the proportion of time that a child spends at primary school is reduced. One consequence of these changes is that primary schooling takes on more and more of a preparatory character. Unlike the elementary schools of the early twentieth century, modern primary schools are under much less social pressure to provide the rudiments of a complete education. As 'first' schools, their main concern is with 'early' education. To the degree that the primary school curriculum has been affected by these trends, its concerns are now much closer to those of middle-class 'preparatory' schools of an earlier era.

Recently, however, a new and confounding element has entered the debates. The preparatory role of the primary school has been rendered very unstable by the current rates of social and educational change. In practice it has become extremely difficult to agree upon a suitable curriculum for the primary school: the pattern of future events is too unpredictable.

This inherent instability in the primary school curriculum is reflected in the way it has responded to the fads and fashions of educational innovation. Although vaccilations of this kind are sometimes considered to be one of primary education's chronic weaknesses, they can also be regarded as one of its enduring strengths. The readiness with which unworkable or outdated techniques have been dropped from the primary school curriculum suggests that it has developed a degree of open-ness and flexibility which, until recently, has been absent from the higher reaches of the education system.

A second influence on the primary school has come from the growth of pre-schooling. In one sense this development undermines the curriculum of primary education by pre-empting some of its traditional tasks. In a different sense, however, pre-schooling has (or can have) an enhancing effect. It can provide children with some of the basic social, intellectual, and emotional skills that are necessary for the successful organisation of the primary school. Although such skills (eg, the ability to share resources, to listen to a story, and to survive for extended periods away from home) may seem trivial, their acquisition can take up a large part of a child's first year at school.

A third development in primary education relates to a changing conception of knowledge. The teaching of reading provides an illustration. It is commonly stated that the purpose of teaching children to read is to introduce them to the 'world of print'. Not much more than one hundred years ago the world of print was comparatively small. For most Scottish school-children it revolved round the Bible—a book with a finite vocabulary. Today, however, the world of print has become an expanding universe. As such, reading is no longer simply a case of word recognition.

In short, the modern requirement is not only to teach children reading (a passive process) but also how to read (an activity which allows them to go beyond their available knowledge). As this example suggests, primary schooling is not so much about teaching facts as about teaching children how to learn. The three Rs are still central to this process but they take on a different role. They are the raw materials, not the finished product; they are the means to an end, not the end in itself.

A fourth influence on primary education arises from the fact that there are fewer prior grounds for stressing one area of the curriculum rather than another. This has not always been the case. In the nineteenth century, for example, the demand for literate clerks and numerate shop assistants helped to shape the elementary school curriculum unambiguously around the three Rs. Nowadays the situation has changed. A child's future vocation is much less easy to predict. In effect, modern primary schools have to take account of adult careers that do not yet exist. This uncertainty is reflected within the school setting by a greater concern for the whole curriculum or, as it is sometimes expressed, the 'whole' child.

Such attention is also focused by a growing belief that children can learn from many different sources and in many different ways. From this viewpoint, for example, painting is not simply to be regarded as an aesthetic experience; it also provides opportunities for muscular coordination (essential for writing), for the appreciation of space and scale (mathematics), and for the differentiation of colour and tone (vocabulary). To the extent that every activity contributes to every other activity, the boundaries of the primary school curriculum are relatively arbitrary. In practice, therefore, it is educationally much easier to justify the inclusion of an activity than to demonstrate its irrelevance. Again this tends to make the primary school curriculum much more open and all-embracing.

Finally, research on child development has had a profound influence on primary education. For many years— to cite a trivial instance—it has been recognised that children usually learn to crawl before they learn to walk. More recently, a comparable level of understanding has been reached with respect to a child's intellectual growth. It is now more widely realised, for example, that children must be able to distinguish shapes before they can learn to read, that they must have a sense of two-dimensional space before they can appreciate a map, and that they must be able to differentiate volume and weight before they can develop a concept of density. Clearly, information about developmental learning has had a considerable impact on the organisation of the primary school curriculum. In particular it has led to a much closer integration of the various elements. The teaching of reading provides a further illustration. It is now unfashionable to use the concept 'reading readiness'—a view which implied that reading could be separate from other activities of the curriculum. Nowadays it is usual to acknowledge the contributory influence of other literacy-related activities by referring to them as 'pre-reading skills'.

IN THE REALM OF PRACTICE

Above and beyond their influence on the primary school curriculum, the external factors described above have also had an impact in the way teachers behave and on the way schools are equipped and designed.

Primary school curricula that aim to encourage intellectual flexibility, cannot rely upon closed teaching methods to achieve this end. 'Drill and practice' may be an efficient way to transmit factual knowledge but it is a much less effective technique for fostering curiosity and self-assurance. Similarly, didactic class teaching (ie, lecturing) is a clumsy if not contradictory method for teaching the kind of skills required of an independent but flexible mind. Once again, the teaching of reading provides a practical illustration. Children can be taught to 'bark at print' by means of class teaching, but need a much more personalised or interactive form of tuition before they can 'read for comprehension'. As this example suggests, the development of new curricula also requires the formulation of new teaching methods. In the case of the open-plan school, the groundswell of change takes the form of a move away from class teaching as the dominant mode of instruction towards an increased reliance on personalised forms of tuition. Note, however, a withdrawal of class teaching does not guarantee a move towards more personalised methods. Indeed, the reverse can be true. Whole-group teaching, for instance, can be highly personalised (especially if the teacher and class have known each other for a long time). Likewise, individual tuition can be highly impersonal (as in programmed learning).

In certain aspects, the emergent personalised methods of the primary school bear a close resemblance to those of an Oxbridge tutorial. Their social setting, however, is fundamentally different: primary education is organised on the basis that teachers and pupils work together for most of the school day whereas university education requires that lecturers are responsible for their students for only relatively short periods. Furthemore, university tutorials are usually conducted privately, not, as it were, in the middle of a crowded lecture hall. These contextual differences have an important consequence for the organisation of tutorial methods in a primary school. Before school teachers can implement such methods they must first consider the activities of their entire teaching group.

Thus, to establish and preserve the 'privacy' of their tutorials, primary school teachers must first design a core of activities which the rest of their children can follow without direct supervision. Second, they must devise methods for monitoring their pupils' progress by indirect rather than direct means (eg, through the use of self-correcting apparatus). Third, they must plan a layout for the class area so as to make equipment accessible and pupil circulation possible. And finally, to achieve an uninterrupted flow of events they need to develop work schedules that allow children to switch easily from group activities to individual tuition. This type of preparation is essential to the successful implementation of tutorial methods in a primary school. It is, however, only part of the story. The day-by-day tactics of teachers also pre-suppose a set of long-term goals related to the overall social, emotional, and intellectual development of their pupils. The formulation of these strategic goals is a teaching task that cannot be realised over-night. It requires the wisdom of experience rather than the virtue of preparation. Just as the running of a home is much more than the making of beds and the planning of menus, so the organisation of primary school teaching is much more than the marking of books and the selection of reading schemes.

The development of tutorial methods also requires a high level of independence and responsibility among the children in a teaching group. These pupil attributes complement those of the teacher. They are not, however, entirely separate. If children do not possess these skills then their realisation must be a necessary part of the teacher's overall planning. For instance, before children can follow a tutorial system they need to learn where equipment is stored, how it should be replaced, where they should put their books to be marked; what they should do if they want to go to the toilet and, not least, how to control the sound of their own voices.

As noted earlier, an open curriculum also requires a much more varied and extensive provision of resources. There is no point, for instance, in introducing children to the world of print if they are simultaneously denied the resources of a library. Likewise, if it is considered important that pupils should exercise choice, then they must be offered a range of realistic alternatives. In a very real sense, therefore, the curriculum of a primary school hinges on the contents of the teacher's store cupboard.

Resources are also important in other ways. A generous supply of space (eg, for pupil circulation) and ample provision of time (eg, for teacher preparation) are also connected with the successful development of tutorial methods.

Not surprisingly, a curriculum that stresses personalised teaching methods can also benefit from additional human resources. In recent years this extra human capital has been created in various ways. Most important has been the gradual reduction of pupil-teacher ratios. Clearly, tutorial methods are more feasible with smaller teaching groups.

A second way of increasing human resources relates to the redistribution or refurbishing of existing capital. Team teaching and cross teaching[2] are examples of the reallocation of instructional resources; and in-service training is a clear example of teacher renewal.

[2] Ie, exchange of classes by teachers.

Human capital can also be created by introducing new personnel into a teaching situation. To the extent that classroom assistants can relieve the teacher from certain routine activities, they inevitably create more time for the teacher to work on lesson preparation and tutorial teaching. Furthermore, teachers and auxiliaries can jointly protect the privacy of the tutorial situation. If children need certain kinds of help, they can be taught by the teacher to go directly to an auxiliary.

Pupils provide a fourth kind of human resource. By helping each other, children can supply much of the assistance that might otherwise come from teachers and auxiliaries. Pupil cooperation however, does not emerge in a vacuum. It requires, for example, careful but indirect supervision on the part of the teacher and a suitable setting for the pupils to gain access to each other.

As the preceding paragraphs suggest it is relatively easy to find links between various kinds of curricula and teaching methods. School design, however, is a little more difficult to integrate. There is no simple one-to-one relationship between an open curriculum and an open-plan school. For instance many of the assumptions outlined above have been brought to life in old classroom schools. What, then, is the meaning of 'purpose-built open-plan design'?

Probably the easiest way to make the connection is to consider the way in which educational materials become essential parts of the primary school curriculum. When the classroom school came into being towards the end of the nineteenth century many resources (eg, books, water) were considered peripheral to the daily work of teachers and pupils. As a result they were usually located quite apart from the individual classroom in communal store cupboards and cloakrooms.

Nowadays, the increased importance of material resources means that they must be located much closer to the child's regular working milieu. However, at any given time, certain items are too costly to be made available in every classroom or to every child. In short, such items become shared rather than guaranteed resources. Thus, to make such limited materials easily available, it is important that they are made readily accessible. In part, access is an architectural problem which can be overcome by the removal of doors and walls and by the revision of building regulations. One of the teachers in the case-study school highlighted the significance of these factors when she said 'My teaching methods haven't changed (since I moved into the new building), but *it's so handy.*' Nevertheless, it is also true that the design of the case-study school did not overcome all problems related to access. An interview study revealed that the children whose class areas bounded the courtyards were four times more likely to have been out-doors than children whose class areas were further away. (No class areas, however, was more than eight metres from a courtyard door.)

To this degree, the development of open-plan schools is not so much an educational response to a change in teaching methods as an architectural response to a greatly increased use of specialist plant and equipment.

CONCLUSION

This essay has tried to explicate and inter-relate some of the diverse notions and activities that characterise recent developments in open-plan schooling. Whether these ideas are widely implemented or even fully accepted is, of course, a separate question. Certainly, critics of primary education have been quick to exploit any apparent discrepancies between the aspirations of educationalists and the practices of teachers. Sometimes the educationalists are blamed, sometimes the teachers and their pupils. Nevertheless, as this essay indicates, such explanations are inadequate. The successes and failures of schooling are rarely the sole responsibility of any one group in education. For instance, the implementation of tutorial teaching in a primary school demands much more than well-trained and skilful teachers. Without a generous supply of equipment, space, and preparation-time and without the kind of additional support offered by auxiliaries, its potential will always remain unfulfilled. Likewise, all the resources in the world cannot establish a given curriculum unless teachers, pupils, parents, and others begin to acknowledge, understand, and share the assumptions on which it is based.

Open-plan schooling, like any other kind of schooling, is not simply a cluster of theoretical assumptions, still less a set of individual practices. Its realisation is a combination of both practice and theory. If the teacher's task in education is to translate theory into practice, it is the researcher's task to translate practice into theory. In so far as the case-study school attempted the former, these essays have tried to accomplish the latter.

BIBLIOGRAPHIC NOTE

In Search of Structure: Essays from an Open-Plan School is a revised version of a report to the Educational Research Board of the Social Science Research Council (Grant No HR 3455). The full report—which also contains additional methodological and bibliographic material—can be obtained on loan from the British Library Lending Division. It can also be purchased on microfiche, (under the title, *A Case Study of a New Scottish Open-plan School*), from the Educational Research Information Center (ERIC) documentation service (ERIC document number ED 128070).

As noted in the introduction, a central concern of these essays was to keep them concise but open ended. No claim, therefore, is made that they provide a definitive statement or even that they encompass all the issues raised during the course of the research. Certainly there are many practical and theoretical questions still to be addressed. The debate has hardly begun.

For anyone interested in taking a second look at the ideas surrounding open-plan schooling, the BBC booklets *Early Years at School* (1973) and *State of Play* (1975) provide excellent starting points and comprehensive bibliographies. Also there are a number of recent publications which offer a more critical appraisal of British Primary Education. None of these would be considered light reading, yet each one merits serious consideration. They include:

- R S Peters (editor), *Perspectives on Plowden* (London: Routledge & Kegan Paul, 1973).
- R Nash, *Classrooms Observed* (London: Routledge & Kegan Paul, 1973).
- B Bernstein, 'Class and pedagogies: visible and invisible' in B Bernstein, *Class Codes and Control,* Vol 3 (London: Routledge & Kegan Paul, 1975).
- R Sharp and A Green, *Education and Social Control* (London: Routledge & Kegan Paul, 1975).
- N Bennett, *Teaching Styles and Pupil Progress* (London: Open Books, 1976).

INDEX

Act for Settling Schools, 1696, 24
Advisers, 35

BBC, bibl.
Bennett, N, bibl.
Bernstein, B, bibl.
Blackboard, 1, 26, 55, 83, 87, 93
Bruner, J, 98
Building Costs Limits, 33

Catechism, 26, 27
CLASP School Design, 4, 33
Class—Boundaries, 44, 45
  Size, 10, 19
Class Codes and Control, bibl.
Classroom Rules, 40, 41, 47, 50, 55, 87
Colleges of Education, 9, 35, 71
Complexities of an Urban Classroom, The, 65
Corrie, Malcolm, preface
Crisis in the Classroom, 39

Department of Education & Science (DES), 8, 20, 21
Design of English Elementary and Primary Schools, 37
Dinner Party Curriculum, 46, 53, 61
Durkheim, Emile, 23
Dux, 26

Early Years at School, bibl.
Edinburgh High School, 25
Education and Social Control, bibl.
Educational Institute of Scotland (EIS), 8
Educational Research — Strengths; Weaknesses, 1; 2
Educational Standards, 18
Educational Values, 6, 20
English Primary Education and the Progressives, 70
Enstein, Albert, preface
Eveline Lowe School, 34, 68
Evolution of the Nursery-Infant School, 1800-1970, The, 37

Finmere School, 33
Froebel, Friedrich, 76
Froebel Certificate, 36

Grant, J, 68
Guide to Classroom Observation, A, 65

Her Majesty's Inspectors, 30, 32
History of the Burgh and Parish Schools of Scotland, 68
History of the Scottish People, A, 36
Homework, 87, 89, 94
Hutted Operation for the Raising of the School Leaving Age, 31, 32, 34

In-service Training, 35, 63

Jackson, P W, 65

Kirkhill School, 34, 68
Knox, John, 24

Leach, Edmund, 8
Life in Classrooms, 65
Literate Curriculum, 27, 55, 92

McNicholas, J, 37
Milk, 43, 49, 55, 73, 77, 78, 83
Ministry of Education Development Group, 32
Monitorial System, 23, 29, 30
Montessori, Maria, 76
Moral Education, 28
Morrell, Derek, 32

Nash, R, bibl.

Open-Plan Organisation in the Primary School, 67

Parents, 17, 25, 40, 49
Perspectives on Plowden, bibl.
Peters, R S, bibl.
Piaget, Jean, 1
Plowden Committee, 34
Policies of School Building Design, 69
Pre-reading Skills, 102
Pre-schooling, 36, 76, 100
Primary Education in Scotland (SED Memorandum), 34
Pupil Chairs, 14, 25, 58, 66, 93, 96
Pupil Grouping, 11, 12, 47, 51, 53, 54, 66, 68, 69, 73, 92, 93
Pupil-Teacher Ratio, 31, 98

Queueing, 58

Researcher Competence, 3
Reformation, Scottish, 23, 24
Raising of School Leaving Age, 32, 99
Rintoul, K, and Thorne, K, 67

St Andrews Grammar School, 67, 73
School Day, Length of, 12, 14, 27, 28, 96, 98
School Furniture, 14, 50, 63, 68
School Size, 30, 31
Schools:
    Adventure, 28
    Charitable, 28
    Elementary, 31, 99
    Grant-aid, 9
    Monitorial, see monitorial system
    Open-plan, 36, 67
    Parochial, 25, 27, 28, 36
    Nursery, 41, 49, 58, 76
    Sessional, 29
    Subscription, 28
Secondary School Selection, 33
Secular Education, 28
Sharp, R, and Green, A, bibl.
Shorter Catechism, The, 26
Self-Service Curriculum, 55

Selleck, R J W, 70
Silberman, Charles, 39
Skilbeck, Malcolm, 75
Smith, L M, and Geoffrey, W, 65
Smorgasbord Curriculum, 46, 61
Smout, T, C, 36
Social Science Research Council, preface
Space for Learning, preface
State of Play, bibl.
Structure
    Educational, 3
    Architectural, 4
System Building, 33

Teacher Competence, 3, 62, 65
Teaching
    Personalised, 42, 45, 60, 62, 103
    Tutorial, 103, 104, 105, 106
Teaching Styles and Pupil Progress, bibl.
Theory and Practice, 2, 3, 67, 106

Walker, R, and Adelman, C, 38
Werner, G M, 69
Westbury, Ian, 66
Whitbread, Nanette, 37